THE NATIONAL MODERNIZATION ACT

How to achieve clean energy, climate stability, infrastructure improvements, abundant jobs and how to pay for it

Sage Rainbow

THE NATIONAL MODERNIZATION ACT: HOW TO ACHIEVE CLEAN ENERGY, CLIMATE STABILITY, INFRASTRUCTURE IMPROVEMENTS, ABUNDANT JOBS AND HOW TO PAY FOR IT

META INSIGHT PUBLISHING
3101 Peninsula Road
Suite 314
Channel Island Harbor
Oxnard, CA 93035

ISBN: 1547053569
ISBN 13: 9781547053568

THIS IS DEDICATED TO ALL OF US

I give heartfelt gratitude to all the researchers, journalists, and members of nonprofit organizations who have sincerely dedicated years—and in many instances decades—to informing the public. I would not have been able to compose this initiative without them.

I give special thanks to TW Hawk for his guidance in striving for clarity and truth, and to Kristen for her cogent editorial recommendations.

PREFACE

It has been said that if you find yourself stuck in a hole, the first thing to do is stop digging. Our political system is mired in a deep hole yet Congress continues to dig. This National Modernization Act (NMA) offers Congress a ladder to climb up from the hole to enact bipartisan legislation that fulfills our nation's vital needs. It can also help end the opposition of the parties and foster unity in Congress for the good of our country.

The American bald eagle, thanks to our Founding Fathers, is our symbol of strength and power. It has majestic beauty, great strength and flies high. Since 1782, the eagle has been on the Great Seal of the United States. Its beak holds a banner inscribed with *E Pluribus Unum*, "Out of Many, One." The same image appears on our dollar bill, on the Seal of the Presidency, the Seal of the Supreme Court and across many other government institutions. It signifies that the United States was formed as "a cohesive single nation," per our Founding Fathers, resulting from thirteen colonies joined together. Fifty states are now unified as one nation, but are not acting as a "cohesive single nation."

The eagle has a right wing and left wing as we have the political "wings" of our two parties. It is imperative that both wings work together in order for America to soar. It is impossible for the eagle or our nation to take flight — and to stay aloft — with only one wing dominating, as Congress has demonstrated. For the good of our country, this National Modernization Act provides a cohesive vision to get the wings of the eagle working together to keep our nation aloft and to ascend to greater heights.

The vision is to implement Congressional legislation that establishes clean, safe, renewable energy sources; moderates climate change; introduces a pollution-free vehicular transportation system; improves our roads, bridges, and tunnels; creates a universal electric-power delivery system with an updated national grid; incorporates an employment training and placement program to create and increase jobs; and includes a practical way to fund it all.

That may sound ambitious, but these goals have already been initiated in our culture and in Congress, albeit only in part and with many false starts. This initiative provides a coordinated, holistic approach to fulfilling those goals and is intended for all Americans, as well as for those who represent us.

A personal note:
This initiative will need a political consensus to become a legislative act of Congress. The majority of voters must express their will to Congress and encourage them to act in our best interest. After the last significant electoral cycle, we must ensure that political rhetoric does not distract us from fulfilling a vital common purpose; hopefully, this initiative will succeed and set our country in a more unified direction to act together for the common good.

I am not affiliated with any political party—I have voted as an Independent for decades, casting my vote based on the character and qualifications of each candidate. As a father and grandfather, I am only one concerned citizen reaching out to you, my fellow Americans, with a plan and a message of realistic hope. And, like you, I have to make a choice at election time. I plan to support the candidates who support this initiative.

To date, I have worked 100 percent solo—as a *beneficial* lone wolf of sorts—to compose this initiative. I do not have the financial or networking means at this time to sufficiently propagate it. But I believe strongly in the importance of this issue, I believe that many others who are reading this feel the same way, and I ask those who do have the means to spread the word.

It is my hope that all political parties will embrace these concepts. It is also my hope that a true spirit of cooperation will blossom and will propel our civilization forward to better ways of thinking and acting for the common good. I long for a time of cooperation and a time when greater numbers of people can be *for* something rather than merely *against* something else. The NMA offers a win-win strategy.

I know some people may label me a naïve dreamer, but I fervently feel that this initiative will be a significant step toward advancing our quality of life. I hope that the enactment of this initiative and the means to achieve it will also be an opportunity to foster further cooperation on other important issues. That is my dream. It is my hope that you will share this dream and help make it a reality.

I thank you for your consideration.

* It has been suggested that readers may want to know about my background and motivation for presenting this initiative. I feel I am only the messenger with a patriotic sense of duty, and that it is the message that is paramount, not me. However to assuage those interested and to avoid any distraction caused by those wondering how my name came to be, I have added a bio in the last section - ABOUT THE AUTHOR.

I have used the metaphor of how the biological systems of our body functions relative to how the different parts of this initiative integrate holistically with each other. In delivering state of the art Complementary and Alternative Medical therapies to my patients for over 50 years, I have developed a holistic approach that has proven highly successful. It is my hope that this initiative applied in the same fashion will also prove successful.

CONTENTS

INTRODUCTION

E ach section contains essential conceptual and factual elements, the bricks and mortar needed for Congress to construct a legislative bill for The National Modernization Act (NMA). The pertinent scientific facts are presented to inform you and enable you to determine your own conclusions. That knowledge is also intended to inspire you and others to talk about the issues with conviction and to spur your representatives to act.

A simple way to understand this initiative is to relate it to your body and its individual systems, which must work together in harmony for your body to function.

I.   Transportation vehicles, in this analogy, are similar to the red blood cells in our circulatory system. Our red blood cells pick up and drop off elements we need to sustain our body; in a like fashion, cars, trucks, and buses deliver food supplies, transport us to work or school, and fulfill our other life-sustaining needs.

II. Infrastructure is compared with the circulatory system our blood cells travel through, as we travel in our vehicles on our nation's roadways, bridges, and through tunnels. To maintain our health and roadways, all of our passageways must be unobstructed and safe.

III. Energy is essential. It powers our bodies and is derived from the metabolic processing that converts the food we eat to create energy. Energy that powers our civilization and lights our world is presently derived primarily from the processing and combustion of fossil fuels. It is vital that the sources of food we consume have the least amount of toxicity possible; it is also vital that the sources and methods we use to obtain and utilize our energy produce minimal toxic side effects to our environment and ourselves.

IV. The electric grid is like our nervous system, which interconnects with all the parts of our body and transmits electrical impulses to all of our organs and muscles. Our national system of electrical networks—the grid—delivers energy to our homes and industries. In both our body and our society, it is vital to maintain consistent connectivity.

V. The environment creates our climate conditions. Our atmosphere is like the skin that surrounds our body, which provides insulation, helps regulate our body temperature, and protects us from microbial infections. Our atmosphere surrounds us, regulates our planet's temperatures, and protects us from many hazards large and small—from meteors to ultraviolet radiation. Most importantly, it sustains us with breathable air and potable water that absolutely must be kept healthy to keep us healthy.

VI. All the cells in our body have a unique job necessary for the whole body's healthy functioning, and each of our individual cells must be able to fulfill that role; likewise, each worker needs to use his or her unique abilities in a job to help maintain a healthy economy for our whole nation. Workers must also be able to maintain their individual economic health. Just as the collective health of our individual cells determines our overall health, the collective economic health of workers determines the wealth of our nation. Human energy is our most valuable source of energy.

VII. Our individual will is a psychological force and moral aspect of our humanity. It governs the words we speak and actions we take; our collective wills need to govern our national actions with mutually beneficial goals in order to establish and maintain harmonious functioning of our society. A collective win/win will is the goal and the surest way to succeed.

VIII. Our body depends on an efficient metabolic system to convert nutrients in our food and energize the cellular structures that compose our organs and muscles. The funding for this initiative is like a nutrient source that we can convert into new and updated infrastructures, clean energy, and more jobs to fuel our economy. Neither nutrients for cellular structures nor money used for our infrastructure are wasted; both of those nutrient sources are converted to repair and build physical structural assets that we benefit from. Today's historically low interest rates make this an opportune time to fund this initiative and make a smart investment in our structural assets and our economy.

All of the above functions are needed and must work together to keep our body healthy and strong. All the above NMA initiative functions are also needed and must work together to keep our nation healthy and strong. That is why the functions of this initiative are addressed in a holistic manner to be commonly understood and implemented in complementary ways by an act of Congress.

CHAPTER 1

OUR TRANSPORTATION SYSTEM AND YOUR TRANSPORTATION VEHICLE

I t's eight fifteen on a Monday morning. You're showered, dressed, and ready for your workday in the heart of a densely populated city thirty miles from your home. You go to your studio and get a glass of juice from the small fridge or hit the brew button for a cup of fresh coffee. You check the local traffic conditions by punching in your GPS destination. It announces that your expected time of arrival is at 8:45 a.m. You sit in your comfy reclining chair and read the morning paper or watch a morning TV program. After ten minutes, you feel a little sleepy from the weekend's activities and decide to take a short snooze. At 8:40 a.m., your info panel announces that you will be arriving at your destination on time, at 8:45 a.m. Just another average day's commute.

It wasn't mentioned that after you checked the traffic conditions, you also pressed the proceed button, causing your studio to detach from its docking station at the side of your house. Your "studio" should really be called a TM—a *transportation module* that you can drive or use in hands-free mode. If your TM was not attached to your home, it might have first been summoned from a garaged area or automatically retrieved from street parking. It might be a robot taxi that was automatically hailed. In the future, electric, hands-free TMs will be internally appointed according to your individual taste and budget, from basic to ultra-plush. Travel will be much safer, less costly, and less polluting. Your private TM can even include a voice-operated "chauffeur"; when you issue the command, "Home, James," you'll receive the TM's response: "With pleasure." Trucks and commercial vehicles, as well as buses and recreational vehicles for families on long-haul vacations, will have similar advantages.

But could this really be possible? After all, present rush-hour traffic in large metropolitan areas averages twenty miles per hour. The National Transportation Board states that 86 percent of people rely on cars to get to work. A thirty-mile trip presently takes a stressful and frustrating ninety minutes of stop-and-go driving that pollutes far more than driving at a fixed speed, wastes expensive fuel, and causes a huge loss of productivity and quality of life: a thirty-mile commute demands three hours of round-trip driving time a day—fifteen hours a week, and sixty hours a month. That's like having another unpaid part-time job in addition to your regular work. Commuters living farther away spend even more time and money for fuel.

Transportation modules presently on the road and in development are intended to improve the safety and expensive operation of today's trucks and other commercial vehicles—no more drivers falling asleep at the wheel on twenty-hour hauls. Trucking fills almost all of our consumption needs, from the food we eat to our building supplies to the clothes on our backs, and must operate at the highest safety standards.

Self-driven vehicles will also serve senior citizens and individuals with disabilities. There is a huge loss of independence when one cannot go about freely. When TMs are the norm, people, including those with disabilities, will be able to get around with an unprecedented level of safety. A few years ago, Google released a video of a successful trial run: the film shows a blind man going to a local drive-through restaurant and then picking up dry cleaning without any difficulty.

This technology is becoming increasingly necessary as huge numbers of "baby boomers" will soon be reaching the age when night driving becomes difficult. Some older drivers will choose not to drive at night, but others will, increasing their chances of causing an accident. Even if you're an excellent driver, that won't make any difference if another motorist looks down at his or her texting screen, crosses over the road midline, and collides head-on into you and your family. Avoiding such mishaps is critical, and robocars will allow freedom of movement and create safer roads for everyone.

This future transportation scenario is not only possible but is already in the making; however, it is lacking a fully coordinated implementation plan. Early prototypes of self-driving cars have already gone cross-country, with over a million miles logged. Robotrucks have also accomplished long hauls safely. Many newer cars already on the road have parallel self-parking capabilities, radar and laser detection systems that calculate safe or dangerous distances from cars or pedestrians, automatic braking to prevent collisions, blind-spot detection, and GPS mapping. Manufacturers are already developing vehicle-to-vehicle (V2V) communications systems, which allow cars to exchange information regarding their locations, the directions they are headed in, and their speed. Projecting today's technological advancements forward ten years, there is no doubt that far safer, less expensive, faster, and cleaner transportation—mass, private, and commercial—will become a reality. All developed and developing countries face the same challenges, and many are already seeking similar solutions.

How will self-driven TMs cut down on travel time if there are too many cars on the road now? Future TM transport systems will have cars moving much faster, with calibrated distances between them to maintain safe traffic. Cars equipped with adaptive cruise control are presently on the road and will automatically speed up or slow down at a programmed distance when following another car. New technology could halve the safe distance between transportation modules, effectively doubling a six-lane highway or freeway to twelve. TMs will initially occupy single lanes now dedicated to multiple-passenger vehicles, expanding to additional lanes as this legislative act progresses. TMs will still offer the option of our present manual driving capabilities and should not restrict hands-on driving on the open road. Those who choose to drive their own vehicles will do so in their designated lanes.

Self-driving vehicles will lower insurance rates and bring about a significant reduction in costly repairs, injuries, and deaths. Even at this early stage, automatic braking systems have reduced costly collisions by 14 percent. Presently, 90 percent of road accidents are caused by human error. Evolving accident prevention technology will significantly reduce that unacceptable and dangerous percentage.

Another huge cost-saving benefit will be the option of enjoying all the features above without the expense and upkeep of owning a car. Most cars sit idle for the overwhelming majority of the day and night. You may still want to own your car, but you will also have the option of having a self-driven "taxi" come to your location and take you where and when you want to go. You won't have to refuel or recharge or pay for parking, car insurance, or costly repairs and maintenance. Instead of monthly car-loan payments or lease payments, you'll only have to pay the robotaxi fare when you need it. Autonomous carpool pickup and drop-off routes can also be programmed to share rides, further reducing transportation costs.

The thought of being transported by a driverless vehicle might feel too futuristic—or just too strange—to many people, including myself, but this trend has already started and is moving rapidly ahead. It might feel uncomfortable being a passenger in a car with no driver for the first time, but after the hundredth time, it will seem entirely routine. To get to that point, however, the safety factor must be supreme.

"Safety as supreme" practices have been applied successfully for many decades in our air transportation systems. It is not unusual for people flying in a plane for the first time to be a little nervous. However, after many flights, most people can relax and read a book, watch a movie, eat a meal, take a snooze, or even go to the bathroom while their air vehicle is thirty thousand feet above the earth and traveling at five hundred miles per hour on automatic pilot. We feel comfortable flying because airplane accidents are rare compared to car accidents, as is proven by hundreds of millions of passengers who have safely traveled billions of air miles.

Consider this: when an airplane crashed into the ocean and disappeared off the coast of Malaysia, the world was transfixed. "What went wrong?" people around the globe wondered. "How could this have happened?" Those questions arose because we have come to expect that all possible safety precautions to prevent accidents have been taken. Most airplane accidents grab headlines because those accidents are a rare occurrence. On the other hand, a five-car accident on a highway may not even get a paragraph in the newspaper; it is a daily occurrence and nothing unusual.

Way before the end of this century, vehicular accidents will also become a rarity. Advanced, satellite-programmed guidance systems will insure supreme safety for our ground transportation systems as they now do for air transportation. This doesn't mean that there will never be accidents, but the present driving statistics that tally tens of thousands of deaths and millions of injuries a year due to vehicular accidents in the United States alone will improve dramatically. In 2015 the National Highway Traffic and Safety Administration estimated costs of road accidents at a staggering $230 billion, which is 2.3 percent of our gross national domestic product. The National Modernization Act (NMA) is intended to bring those tragic road statistics to a fraction of their present toll and simultaneously create zip lanes where your transportation module will travel faster than today's speed limit.

Future TMs will have hazard detection systems to always protect you from running over a person, colliding with another vehicle, or an unseen object on the road. The hazard protection system will act as a force field surrounding your car that automatically brakes itself and comes to a stop before impacting anything.

National guidelines are needed to coordinate all these ongoing advancements; lack of centralized coordination is likely to result in conflicting agendas and delay full implementation. Funding to develop and advance our future transportation vehicles is now being provided mainly by auto manufacturers. It will be necessary for the government to support this initiative financially and to coordinate the development of safety measures and a common traffic flow grid standard that can be applied nationally.

The implementation of the NMA must also result in nonpolluting standards for all road vehicles; gasoline and electric fueled. The eventual goal is zero tailpipe emissions fueled with electricity produced with zero pollution renewable energy sources establishing a zero carbon footprint. (Clean energy production is addressed in a following section.) This aspect concerning transportation relative to clean energy is noted here in part because all aspects of this initiative are intertwined and must work in concert to achieve the overall desired results of the NMA.

Major drawbacks to buying an electrical vehicle (EV) are; limited mileage ranges and availability of charging stations. Governments and municipalities need to mandate and/or subsidize a progressive increase in public access to charging stations, such as at shopping plazas, and residential and office buildings. Those who live in a condominium/apartment, like myself, have a common garage or have to park on the street where there is no place to recharge. That precludes most people buying an EV. For extended driving there are not adequate road recharging facilities available, which also hinders choosing an EV. Tesla is planning to have 10,000 charging stations operating by the end of 2017, especially for city dwellers that usually don't have garages. It is important to mandate a universal plug and outlet receptacle so all makes of vehicles can use all recharging stations. Eventually recharging stations may become nearly as common as parking meters.

Consider the future advantages of electric vehicles: if you have a plug-in resource where you parked at home or while shopping or at work, you would never have to drive to a gas station to fill up. Your current cost for a gallon of gasoline may range from $2-4 and give you an approximate 25-40 mile range. An electric charge for the same price would give you double to triple or more mileage. That would be equivalent to paying a dollar a gallon for gasoline or less. You would save a lot of money and leave a zero carbon foot imprint. Costly repairs to the many parts of an internal combustion engine would also be zero.

Automobile manufacturers are very aware of those advantages for the consumer. Volvo announced all of its new cars will be partly or fully battery powered by 2019. Jaguar will produce only electric cars in the next few years. BMW, Land Rover, Mercedes-Benz, Volkswagen, Ford and all major manufacturers of automobiles are already producing or will soon be producing electric and/or hybrid vehicles and are planning greater production in the future as consumer demand and government compliance continues to increase. Britain and France, in addition to several other European countries recently announced that by 2040 they will ban all gasoline and diesel powered vehicles. Major cities such as Athens, Madrid, Paris and Mexico City also plan to ban diesel vehicles by 2025. China and India are also switching to implementation of electric vehicles and phasing out gasoline and diesel fueled vehicles. China's goal is to be the number one producer of electric vehicles in the world. That will be a significant milestone when achieved since China and India alone make up nearly 1/3 of the world's population.

Presently, sales of electric vehicles are very tiny because of some of the limitations mentioned above. But the trend to EV's has already begun and its momentum is building like a distant tsunami wave heading toward the shore. Gasoline powered vehicles will be around for quite a while during this transition phase. However, due to governments around the world mandating low and zero-emission pollution and to reduce greenhouse gases, non-polluting vehicles will be the way of the future for other reasons that will be further discussed.

Whatever type of car you are driving today or new car in the future, all cars must drive on roads. TM vehicles, as mentioned, are like the blood cells in your circulatory system. They must travel unimpeded to all parts of your body through your blood vessels; likewise, you need to travel safely and efficiently through the pathways of tunnels, roads, and bridges to your destination. The following section of the NMA addresses those vital transportation pathways and our dire need to repair and update our nation's infrastructure.

CHAPTER 2

OUR INFRASTRUCTURE ROADS, BRIDGES, AND TUNNELS

Major thoroughfares going into and out from cities are called "arteries." Like the arteries in your circulatory system, they must provide safe and unobstructed passage. Just as narrowing of an artery causes diminished circulation to parts of your body, closure of road lanes for repair narrows the pathway and diminishes traffic flow. Arterial blockages cut off all circulation to parts of your body, and road blockages such as those in a state of major disrepair or closing of unsafe tunnels or bridges will continue to cut off total travel on those passageways until remedied.

If your circulatory system reaches an advanced state of deterioration, your quality of life will be very tenuous. Unfortunately, our infrastructure is presently in that dire state of deterioration. This diagnosis has been arrived at by a multitude of experts in the field, and now has become a critical issue.

How critical is it? *One in three roads in America are in need of repair.* California's transportation agency says that 41 percent of its roads are presently distressed, and many need serious repairs. A March 2017 status report from the American Society of Civil Engineers found that one in every five miles of America's roads was in poor condition.

They projected that $4 trillion will be lost in commerce because of failure to deliver food produce and goods due to road delays, and $7 trillion will be lost in sales of those products. By 2025, two and a half million jobs will also be lost. Ongoing underinvestment in road repairs has led to crumbling and pothole-infested thoroughfares across the country. This is not only dangerous, but also costly to all car owners everywhere. Damage for repairs or replacements of tires, wheels, and suspensions, due to potholes and cracked pavement cost drivers an average of over seven hundred dollars a year, and also results in higher insurance premiums for everyone.

Nationwide, 142,000 bridges are operating deficiently or are obsolete, and one in four bridges is structurally deficient; one of nine bridges is actually rusting. Fifteen major connecting bridges in Philadelphia have rusted to the extent that pieces of the bridges have fallen off. Blatant structural cracks line their foundation supports. These and many other passages across the nation are crucial for commercial and commuter traffic; closure of these bridges causes great economic hardship. Major rail lines from New England down the East Coast, for example, have to merge and pass through a New York/New Jersey commercial hub on an ancient bridge that needs to be closed for repairs periodically. These closures cost millions of dollars in bottleneck delays, costly overtime, and rerouting resulting in missed delivery targets.

These facts are just the tip of the iceberg. Too many of our roads, bridges, and tunnels are literally crumbling. It is not an issue that Congress needs to investigate or debate; over decades, it has already held numerous hearings and heard testimony from experts, authorities, and federal, state, and local government representatives. And, remarkably, the congressional committees addressing these issues have come to an overwhelming agreement: *there is an immediate need to make these repairs and improvements to our transportation infrastructure.*

However, that's where the agreement ends. Despite numerous "shovel-ready" plans for the work, there is no plan to provide the necessary funding. Spending increases are never popular, but business and labor agree that every $1 billion spent for infrastructure will create tens of thousands of new jobs for blue and white-collar workers. Those people's earnings will pay taxes and inject money into the economy through consumer consumption—creating more jobs. It should also be noted that many of these projects have already been cost structured and are ready to proceed now.

If nothing significant is done, the decay of our infrastructure will precipitously worsen. To put it in perspective, the present state of our vital infrastructure can reasonably be compared to tooth decay. Without appropriate treatment, tooth decay leads to the loss of teeth and to more suffering and dysfunction. Failure to act now will actually increase our debt, because future repairs will only require more extensive work. With inflation, future road repair or replacement costs will be much higher. To do nothing now and pay more later would be like paying a balloon payment on a mortgage after years of devastating accumulated interest.

In actuality, our infrastructure is a matter of national security. If you were diagnosed with narrowing blood vessels that could cause blockages, you would be wise to immediately make the vital changes necessary for your health. Congress has accurately diagnosed our unhealthy infrastructure, and now they must act wisely to make our pathways of travel safe and reliable. The alternative is further deterioration and much higher costs in the future. Preventive road maintenance costs about $100,000 per lane mile. Major rehabilitations cost about ten times that—nearly $1,000,000. Many of our roads, bridges, and tunnels are past their shelf life, and many more are souring every day. It would be wise to act now, while construction materials and commodities are at favorable cyclical lows.

Volumes of transportation studies and testimonies including facts and figures from every state describe the urgent need to take action immediately. These facts are presently a matter of congressional record. Many members of committees such as the House Transportation and Infrastructure Committee are acutely aware of these issues. These facts are intended to elevate awareness and spur voters to urge Congress and the president to take immediate action. It is to be expected that self-serving groups will oppose parts of this project, but with the power of your voice and your vote, those opposing efforts will be overcome—for everyone's benefit. Regardless of political affiliation, everyone drives on the same roads—even presidents. The goal is to have safe, smooth roads for everyone.

A practical example of this modernization act working in a coordinated, holistic way is to install vehicle-to-infrastructure (V2I) sensing/relay devices on our roads, bridges, and tunnels as they are being repaired and updated. V2I devices are similar to V2V (car to car) devices, but they are embedded into roads, bridges, and tunnels to broadcast warnings of lane closures or dangerous conditions and offer alternate routes. They can also help regulate your car's speed so you never have to stop for traffic lights and can avoid stop-and-go braking and acceleration. Safe, fluid, comfortable, and easy road traveling are the goals. This is the smart way to modernize and coordinate TM vehicles with our infrastructure transportation pathways and fulfill the collective goals of this initiative.

There is a saying that "all roads lead to Rome." If Rome hadn't maintained its roads, then trade, commerce, and the movement of their armies would have halted; the empire would not have been able to maintain a vibrant economy for as long as it did. The United States has the world's largest economy, yet we aren't even ranked in the top ten developed nations for good roads. We must have good infrastructure to continue to grow as a country. It is a basic requirement for our nation to safely function. After all, the most important road in the United States is the one you drive on. With our wealth and vast technological prowess, shouldn't we expect our roads to give us safe, smooth, and comfortable rides? We should all want to come together to make this a reality.

Building better roads to physically connect us also presents an opportunity to work together shoulder to shoulder for a common cause and hopefully will also foster a better spiritual connection with each other.

The following section addresses our electric grid. It is another vital organ of our infrastructure in urgent need of updating—failure to do so poses a grave, ongoing danger to our nation. If these terms sound severe, it's because the situation is dire.

CHAPTER 3

OUR ELECTRIC "GRID" INFRASTRUCTURE

S ever a nerve to your arm, and it becomes paralyzed. A blockage or clot in your brain can cause a stroke, which may result in paralysis to half of your body. Without proper transmission, the powerhouse of your brain becomes unable to convey the neuroelectrical messages that enable normal function of your limbs; even your speech can be impaired due to paralysis of your tongue. Our nation's electric grid is somewhat like our neurological system: if there is a failure in the generator, power lines, transformers, or substations supplying electricity to a region, normal living conditions become impossible.

Not too long ago, for example, there was a major blackout in New York City. My son was visiting relatives at the time and had to use his cell phone light to walk up darkened stairs in an apartment building where the electric elevators had failed to operate. Hundreds of thousands of people were affected. Trains were immobile, stranding those dependent on them. Cars were also nearly useless as traffic lights failed to operate, causing insurmountable road blockages that trapped commuters in the city. Many had to book hotels or were forced to sleep on the streets.

Prolonged electric power failure results in paralysis of transportation because gas pumps stop functioning and cars and trucks can't refuel, nor can electric vehicles recharge. Travel to work ceases, and jobs in banking, retail, and almost all commercial activities dependent on electronic cash registers become impossible. Credit-card transactions and business dependent on computers also cease. Commerce comes to a standstill. After your cell phone and computer batteries run down, there will be no electricity to recharge them and no TV to find out what is happening. Those dependent on electric heat will experience very cold, intolerable winters with no cooking on electric stoves. Perhaps the greatest hardship is the lack of food—there are no new food deliveries to replenish stores, and no refrigeration to prevent perishables from spoiling. Once home generators run out of gas, they too become inoperable. Obviously, this catastrophe must be avoided. As has been duly recognized by both houses of Congress, damage to our electric grid is plainly a clear and present threat to our national security.

We depend on the grid to power our homes, our industries, and our ways of living, but many of its vital parts were built in the middle of the twentieth century—or earlier—and are now antiquated and in present danger of failing. Despite Congress's long-standing critical awareness of this danger, no significant action has been taken or money allocated to remedy this dire threat.

Past congressional action on appropriating funds for our electric grid infrastructure calls to mind a homeowner who calls an electrician to investigate intermittent short circuits. The inspection reveals a faulty, outdated wiring system that will only continue to deteriorate and cause future problems—in fact, the decline will accelerate and get worse, and total failure will eventually occur.

Imagine that this is your home. That's obviously terrible news, but common sense would dictate that the electrician do the necessary repairs immediately. But the lights are still on *for now*, so you put it off for a little while because you have other bills to pay. The "little while" turns into a longer while, the short circuits start again, you call another electrician to assess the problem, and again you are told the same thing—only this time the problem is worse. This time, due to further deterioration and increased prices for parts and labor, it will cost a lot more money than before. Basically, this is what Congress has been doing for decades. They have put off the remedy for too long. This present danger now hovers over everyone's home, and our homeland.

Another critical consideration for taking immediate action is the possibility of an electromagnetic pulse (EMP), which would fry our present power grid. An EMP can occur due to a solar storm or be triggered via a strategic device launched by a terrorist or foreign country. This is not mere speculation but a highly authoritative conclusion made by Peter Vincent Pry, Chief of Staff of the Congressional EMP Commission, R. James Woolsey, a former director of the CIA, and the heads of the Strategic Defensive Initiative and the National Intelligence Council. In an article published in the *Wall Street Journal* on February 28, 2017, Mr. Woolsey and Mr. Pry wrote:

> The congressional EMP commission—and Russian, Chinese, and South Korean sources—assess that North Korea probably has nuclear arms specialized for electromagnetic pulse, what Russians call "super-EMP" weapons. These warheads would be low-yield because they are designed to produce gamma rays, not a big explosion.

> These are the most dangerous weapons known to man. A single super-EMP warhead detonated over North America could permanently black out the United States and Canada and kill up to 90 percent of the population through starvation and societal collapse.

Lloyds of London estimated that an electromagnetic pulse could cause between twenty and forty million Americans to lose electricity for up to two years, causing massive riots and crimes committed by desperate people stealing food for their families.

In their closing statements, Mr. Woolsey and Mr. Pry recommended, "The United States should immediately harden its electric grid to deter and defeat a nuclear EMP attack."

An attack by an EMP weapon isn't the only reason to update and harden our electric grid. Solar storms occur naturally, and—like the weather—they can be unpredictable. As recently as July of 2012, a massive solar storm the size of California was unleashed toward earth. Like a speeding bowling ball that narrowly misses its target, the solar storm missed our planet's orbit by only seven days.

This solar event alarmed the American Geological Union and the Federal Energy Regulatory Commission, which urged utility companies to formulate plans for this eventuality. Taken by the startling facts and consequences of such a critical failure, the House of Representatives acted and supported legislation that passed in 2010, but the Senate killed the bill. It would have urged utilities to have spare transformers, extra backup equipment, and blocking capacities to shield key components.

Of course, even without an electromagnetic pulse, cyberattacks can override a facility's computer controls. Simulated tests have demonstrated how a cyberattack could instruct a turbine to operate at excessive speeds until the heat generated caused the turbine's parts to fuse together, destroying it.

Turbines are like a locomotive engine, large and very heavy. When a massive turbine spins at a dangerous accelerated velocity, it starts to vibrate, then shakes wildly on its foundation, then smokes, and finally stops dead, fused, impossible to repair. It takes considerable time to build a new turbine, carefully transport it, and install it so electricity can come online again. A reliable backup and relay system must be put in place to ensure that the flow of electricity to your region will never be interrupted for an unacceptable period of time.

Isn't it just common sense that a family on a long-distance trip has a spare tire in case of a blowout that would leave them stranded? In Congress, tea party Republicans and staunch Democrats both agree that utilities are unprepared in the event of a massive solar storm or cyberattack. However, due to congressional lobbying by electrical utility providers to avoid costs for needed updates, no significant action has been taken. The cost of inaction puts us all in harm's way.

Hopefully, your voice and vote can help spur Congress to sign on to this imperative initiative and get our homeland in proper working order. In the 2016 presidential campaign, both the Republican and Democratic parties advocated for infrastructure funding and implementation in their platforms. Past actions by both parties have echoed similar proclamations before, and if there had been true follow-through, there would be no need to pass this National Modernization Act.

We can't do much when our planet's tectonic plates shift, causing faults that produce earthquakes, but we have fortified the structures of buildings in order to save lives. We cannot prevent solar storms, either, but we can fortify our electric grid structure to prevent massive tragedies. It is within our capacity to do so, and failure to act will perpetuate a grave threat to our nation's way of life.

Our electrical gird connects and delivers our most important energy needs, but it is useless without a reliable energy source. The next section addresses the essential requirements for safe and clean energy production from sustainable resources. It is perhaps the greatest challenge of our times.

CHAPTER 4

ENERGY: OUR SOURCES

This section on energy sources contrasts clean alternative energy with the known toxic health and environmental hazards of fossil-fuel consumption. Climate considerations that address global warming are addressed as a separate issue in the following section. However, even in the absence of global warming data, the hazardous polluting effects of fossil fuel burning are significant enough to mandate a transition to alternative energy sources.

In today's civilization, we require a great deal of energy to sustain our lives. This energy has been predominantly produced by burning coal or oil to boil water in order to turn turbines that generate electricity. The boiling water produces steam that turns turbines, which are encircled with copper wire to produce a "spin-off" flow of electronic impulses like a twirling umbrella spins off water droplets. Those impulses transfer from one electron in a copper wire to another and deliver electricity at the end of the line. Coal and oil are derived from ancient, carbon-based life-forms that have been squeezed for hundreds of millions of years by the massive might of our planet. The amount of oil under the ground is finite and nonrenewable; once a fossil fuel is burned, it cannot be replaced within our lifetime. It is a non-sustainable source of energy.

Oil producers, scientists, and geologists know that in the future, alternative fuels and other means to produce electricity must replace today's use of coal and oil. We also know that because coal and oil are carbon based, they produce carbon dioxide and other pollutants when they are burned. When oil and oil products are distributed, leaking pipelines can emit methane, which is toxic to humans and many times more destructive to our atmosphere than carbon dioxide. There are over 2.5 million miles of energy pipelines in the United States, which will eventually corrode, leak and need replacement.

We already have access to alternative sources of electricity. Solar panels convert sunlight into a form of electrical energy that is safe, clean, and renewable. We are in a very early stage of utilizing this technology, and advancements in its manufacture and installation are continuously bringing down the cost of generating electricity. In growing numbers, solar homeowners are selling extra electricity back to the grid and receiving credits on their electric bills.

Windmills also spin turbines that produce safe, clean, renewable electricity. As long as our planet continues to spin at twenty-four thousand miles per hour, directing wind currents, wind energy will be renewable; even with some windless days, it is a highly reliable source of clean electricity over the months and years. The wind-power industry, like the solar industry, is expanding. In addition to land-based windmills, offshore ocean wind farms are being planned on both coasts, including one thirty miles off the coast of Montauk, Long Island. Ocean winds are usually stronger than land winds and have been broadly used as a source of power in European countries. Wind energy sources contributed 9.9 percent of the European Union's total electricity production in 2016. It has been estimated that wind energy could provide four times more electricity for our future national grid than all present sources do today.

Geothermal energy derived from the earth's interior heat produced 32 percent of California's total renewable energy in 2013, three times the amount produced by solar energy. It has been used in other nations for decades, and it too is safe, clean, and renewable. Other clean and renewable power sources are also currently in use, such as ion exchange fuel cells that produce a flow of electrons to run a car and produce only water as tailpipe exhaust.

It is reasonable to project that clean, safe, renewable technologies and economies of scale will continue to evolve to produce the energy needed for our National Modernization Act. The holistic goal is to have all sources of energy funneled into a national electric grid and distributed to meet all our electric needs. This is another reason that this initiative needs to proceed as a complete package of present and future needs including transportation vehicles, infrastructure, and all energy sources. The key to success is to coordinate all these components in a way that is not piecemeal or watered down in order to achieve the common overall goal.

The bottom line is that we have no better choice. Because burning fossil fuels is toxic, destructive, and not sustainable, the far better choice is to enact this imperative NMA as soon as possible.

What makes this National Modernization Act imperative? Your lungs and their thousands of alveoli sacks. If you were to spread out the lining of your lungs on a flat surface, it would take up an area the size of a tennis court. If you poured a bucket of water over the surface of the tennis court on a hot day, it would quickly evaporate. If you had put a handful of dust sweepings and sand into the bucket beforehand, the evaporated water would leave a residue of sand and dust on the surface of the tennis court.

With each breath you breathe, you take whatever is in the atmosphere into your lungs, breathing in carbon and other particulates along with oxygen and other atmospheric vapors. Many of the carbon particles from soot and other harmful particulates from fossil fuel combustion remain in your lungs just as the sand and dust remains on the tennis court. Inside your lungs, moisture evaporates rapidly with each breath exhaled and concentrates the remaining harmful residue. Cilia in the mucosal lining of your respiratory system help to sweep away some, but not all, of the larger carbon particles. Many of the finer disease-causing particulates can lodge and remain in the lungs, and many of the harmful *vapors* breathed in penetrate the mucosal barrier and are absorbed directly into the bloodstream and carried throughout your whole body, adversely affecting your organs.

Particulates in the air affect our cardiovascular systems and transport carcinogens throughout the body. It has been well documented worldwide that soot particles lead to asthma, cancer of the throat, bronchial and lung diseases, birth defects, premature deliveries, and cardiovascular disease caused by plaque buildup and hardening of the arteries. A 2011 study suggests that heart attacks caused by traffic exhaust could be prevented if the poisonous emissions were eliminated.

Smog consists of sulfur dioxide, nitrogen oxides, carbon monoxide, soot (which is black carbon), and many other disease-causing pollutants. It is the sulfur content of smog that gives it its yellow color. Sulfur dioxide also creates acid rains that damages forests, soils, and crops, and can cause streams and lakes to become acidic and harm aquatic life.

Smog is something that everyone can see—although it might be more accurate to state that smog prevents us from seeing clearly, because the dense particulate matter contained within it diminishes visibility. In 2013, the manufacturing city of Harbin, China was so smog-saturated that people couldn't see their dogs at the end of their leashes. Paris has also been plagued by smog pollution so severe that the Eiffel tower could barely be seen. A driving ban was issued, limiting Parisian car owners to driving only on alternate days—based on their-even or odd-numbered license plates—and with a speed limit of only twelve miles an hour. Similar efforts to reduce the number of cars on the road have been issued in many cities around the world.

When smog concentration reaches levels hazardous to children and people with health problems, they are warned not to go outside. This has occurred in American cities such as Los Angeles, Denver, and Phoenix, and is a recurring problem in other cities around the world, including Athens, Rome, Seoul, Santiago, and Mexico City. These major world cities have also had to resort to alternate driving days, and their citizens are warned *not* to bike or run for health reasons—exercising outdoors requires deeper breathing, causing deeper penetration of the particulates into the lungs. In Beijing, China, the smog-pollution problem has become so prevalent that it is common to see people wearing facemasks to filter out particulates on a daily basis. Manufacturers of facemasks are now producing them with fashionable designs to choose from.

As severe as the smog has been in Beijing, Salt Lake City, Utah surpassed the Chinese city one day in 2013 as having even higher pollution according to the Environmental Protection Agency. Residents wore surgical masks there as well, and many people with children fled to the mountains to escape scratchy throats and itchy eyes.

A June 2017 study by the Harvard T.H. Chan School of Public Health published in *The New England Journal of Medicine* analyzed the air-quality from every part of the continental United States—rural areas and cities alike, divided into one-kilometer areas. The findings revealed that the EPA's current acceptable levels for ozone and fine particulate matter were not safe at all and led to illnesses and premature death among seniors. It was recommended that acceptable standards be set much lower. Francesca Dominici, a data scientist conducting the study observed that, "the air we are breathing right now is harmful, it's toxic."

In China, where cigarette smoking has been on the decline, the rate of lung cancer has ironically *increased*. As industrialization has increased over the last thirty years, so has burning of fossil fuels to power factories—and the rate of lung cancer deaths has risen an astounding 465 percent. The incidence of young children and nonsmokers diagnosed with lung cancer has been dramatic in many industrialized cities. This pollution of major cities has alarmed China's citizens and their government, which seeks to maintain political stability and reduce escalating healthcare costs for pollution-related diseases. China is the world's largest producer of carbon-pollutant emissions; the United States is the second largest, and together both countries produce a whopping 40 percent of the world's emissions. Per capita, the U.S. is the world's biggest polluter.

Despite past hostilities between the two nations, both countries had agreed on a landmark win-win strategy to reduce these emissions. At an official ceremony in 2016, the presidents of both nations committed to work together to reduce greenhouse gases and adopt the Paris Accord as a pragmatic solution. They found common ground because the catastrophic consequences have reached a point that made doing so imperative.

Nearly two hundred other countries belonging to the United Nations also signed on in support of the agreement—Syria passed, and Honduras didn't sign on because it felt the restrictions were not strict enough. Under the terms of the accord, each country was allowed to set its own goals to limit fossil fuel use and to use cleaner energy. The terms of the Accord are not binding, as each country can change its commitments and timetables for any reason.

In June of 2017, during the final editing for this book, the US president planned to pull out of the Paris Accord. Despite this disappointing decision, we as Americans still have the responsibility to reduce the pollutants we produce. It is to our own benefit as well as to the world. If the rest of the world can agree on pragmatic solutions for the common good, we should expect our representatives, despite their differences, to do the same and vigorously support a win-win strategy to pass this imperative National Modernization Act and adapt it as our standard, and stay in the Accord.

There may be people living in rural or remote areas who think that traffic emissions in cities and smog output from factories in industrial areas do not affect them. They would be *dead* wrong. The way the world cooperates—or not—to reduce toxic carbon emissions affects everyone, everywhere.

Our human global population's activities emit twenty-nine billion tons of carbon dioxide and various toxins a year. Volcanoes, by comparison, emit a comparatively scant 0.2–0.3 tons a year. Those voluminous amounts of emitted toxins go into our atmosphere, making something like a blended toxic smoothie. As our planet spins, stirring the air above as hot and cold air masses pump up and down, it blends the different molecular components—good and bad—into our atmosphere. The volcanic ashes of an eruption can cross over continents or oceans in a week and adversely affect people thousands of miles away.

Even dust particles can be carried far and wide by the jet streams—in one case, from the remote Chinese Gobi Desert and Outer Mongolia to the distant top of Yosemite's Half Dome peak. Scientists from the University of California (sponsored by the National Science Foundation) analyzed the geological age, chemical properties, and isotopic contents of Yosemite's dust. It was mixed with Central California dust and determined that 40 percent originated in the Gobi desert. In this case, the natural desert dust contains important nutrients needed for plant growth and is a beneficial result of particles traveling from one continent to another. The research team also concluded that nutrient-laden dust particles from the Sahara Desert were carried by earth's wind currents to feed the far away rainforests of the Amazon.

What is neither natural nor beneficial is the myriad of pollutants from the burning of carbon-based fuels that go into our global atmosphere twenty-four hours a day, every day of the year. Those pollutants are not limited just to their region of origin; they are blended into our planet's atmosphere, adversely affecting all life on all continents.

Mercury, one of the numerous pollutants from burning coal, is a heavy metal. It is called a heavy metal because as a basic element, it does not easily decay and break down without undergoing a nuclear reaction. When heated or exposed to the atmosphere, it forms compounds that are incorporated into the air as invisible vapors. One of the many adverse effects of mercury is its action as a neurotoxin that retards neurological development in babies and children. It can also cause blindness and mental disabilities in adults. Mercury in our blended atmosphere literally rains down everywhere and is absorbed into the land and sea alike. That means our soil absorbs the mercury, as does all the food grown in it and the grass eaten by the animals that produce meat and dairy for our consumption.

Mercury that has rained down on the oceans has already caused enough toxic build-up in sea life that pregnant women have been warned to avoid many species of fish. It has also been found to cause serious health problems to polar bears. Over decades it has been found in the breast milk of Inuit Arctic women and has caused sterility in Inuit men. The Inuit diet—and that of the polar bears—depends on seals and fatty fish, which have high mercury levels due to their own diet of smaller fish and other sea life that have accumulated mercury from other creatures further down the food chain. Each fish eaten by a larger fish increases the accumulated toxicity when it is eaten yet again by another.

Throughout most of the twentieth century, coal miners brought canaries into the mines with them in order to gauge the air quality underground. When the air became too foul to sustain the tiny birds' lives, the canaries' deaths warned the coal miners that they too were in peril and needed to act quickly and get out of danger. Polar bears and the Inuit people have become our planet's symbolic canaries.

The earth's "smoothie blender" works day and night, blending all its airborne ingredients into our atmosphere. Mercury is only one of many toxic ingredients; some fossil fuels, for example, also produce arsenic. Other carcinogenic and disease-causing toxins emitted into our atmosphere from burning fossil fuels include nitrogen oxide, ammonia, carbon monoxide, and sulfur dioxide. Extraction methods to obtain oil also release hazardous toxins such as benzene, formaldehyde, polycyclic aromatic hydrocarbons (PAH), silica, radon, and hydrofluoric acid—a highly dangerous compound that can eat through glass.

If all these contaminants were eliminated, the Environmental Protection Agency estimates that eleven thousand premature deaths would be avoided each year and the incidence of asthma significantly reduced.

We cannot see mercury vapor or the other invisible trace elements we take into our bodies each day, but we can see smog, which should serve as a visible warning. When this National Modernization Act is carried through, you won't have to see any smog or breathe in invisible toxins.

There is an urgent need to make this initiative a reality soon. As mentioned, *twenty-nine billion tons* of man-made carbon emissions are presently put into our atmosphere every year. As the global population continues to grow and economies in developing countries expand, more people will want and do what you want and do. They will be driving far more cars and require much more energy for their industries, office buildings, and homes. Much of the developing world will not be able to afford pollution-reduction devices such as catalytic converters when they desperately need affordable basic transportation, as is the case in India. As a result, the pace at which carbon tonnage is added to our atmosphere will accelerate dramatically.

As a developing country's economy grows, it is an established fact that its energy consumption increases rapidly. China's developing economy has moved four hundred million people out of poverty and into the middle class, but their use of fossil-fuel energy has increased proportionately to make them the world's number-one polluter. China's population continues to grow, and the country's need for energy is growing as well. Add in the rest of the developing world's population seeking the same middle-class status, and you will realize that there will be catastrophic consequences in our future unless we act now.

Together, India and China are home to 2.6 billion of the 7.4 billion people on our planet. Other developing countries in Asia, Africa, and South America are growing as well and also contribute a large share of carbon pollution. The math tells us that twenty-nine billion tons of carbon emissions a year will soon become sixty unless a concentrated effort to slow and reverse this progression is brought to fruition. China has 20 percent of the world's population, and India has 17.13 percent. The United States, in comparison, represents only 4.5 percent of the world's population. With only 350 million people in our country, we are still the world's number-two polluter, and as mentioned, *on a per capita basis, the United States is the world's number one polluter.* With 2.6 billion people in India and China alone working to attain the economic status of our 350 million people, the implications for our environment are severe.

The trends are obvious. Soon India will be the world's second-greatest polluter, moving the United States to third place. In time, they may even become number one. This is a contest nobody wins. In the past, there were times when our nation was pitted against others, enmeshed in an arms race or a space race; now is an opportune time to have a clean-air race. There will be no losers in this contest; it's a win-win for each nation and for our planet.

We've considered many of our energy source options, but there is an outlier that needs to be addressed in this section—nuclear energy. For those of us who share the environmentalist's passion for nature and its preservation, nuclear energy has always been frowned upon. There is the frightening potential for accidents and leakage, in addition to the hazards entailed in transporting and storing nuclear waste that will not decompose within our lifetimes. There is also the possibility of sabotage or a terrorist attack on a nuclear facility.

These dangers need to be acknowledged and carefully considered before we bring new nuclear facilities online. However, there have been new innovations in nuclear technology offering safer possibilities, and this issue should be looked at in a new light. Due diligence in formulating a complete energy package requires that we examine *all* the means at our disposal to produce electricity and decide what compromises are necessary to produce energy in the safest and cleanest ways possible.

Nuclear energy is certainly not 100 percent clean or safe, but neither is burning coal and oil. Nuclear energy, moreover, is sustainable and produces no carbon emissions. New nuclear reactor designs are smaller, can be built much more quickly, and produce more energy at greater efficiency. New ceramic-like materials can better sustain high temperatures, avoiding leakage and meltdowns, and coolants for the new reactors do not require large water supplies and need not be located near an ocean, river, or lake. Only a relatively small amount of fissionable nuclear fuel is needed to produce the large amounts of electrical energy presently produced by fossil fuel burning.

The transportation and storage of radioactive waste has been a huge roadblock for the nuclear industry. No one wants it in their backyard, as has been made clear by vociferous opposition by each state's representatives. This is understandable, given the early "fast breeder" reactors that produced more radioactive waste than was consumed by their plutonium-uranium cores. Catastrophic accidents such as the Chernobyl, Russia meltdown and the Fukushima, Japan tragedy remain as clear warnings. Initial reactors built according to the designs of earlier decades do pose those inherent dangers of tsunami threats and leakage or meltdowns from containment corrosion. However, new reactor designs—*if* proven safely operational—can be placed underground, limiting the effects of any mishap. The new designs also offer the advantage of recycling almost all their nuclear fuel, thus dramatically reducing the need for transportation and storage facilities—and they can run for thirty years without refueling.

We could reduce the threat of a terrorist attack on a nuclear facility by building the new smart reactors on population-remote military bases not located over aquifers. From a strategic point of view, military bases should provide security against terrorist attacks far superior to that of our present facilities. The small amount of nuclear waste produced by the new reactors could be contained in fused-glass barrels and buried in very deep drill-hole wells adjacent to the military bases, which would bring transportation risks to nearly zero.

The Department of Energy has testified to Congress that nuclear energy is vital to accomplishing our goal of low-carbon emissions. These new reactor designs may not prove to be feasible for economic or safety reasons, but the tradeoff question of possible nuclear contamination versus definite carbon pollution needs to be answered. We can eventually obviate the need for all nuclear energy by making other clean, sustainable energy sources more economical. Until then, all energy sources should be carefully considered.

Due to outraged public demand for a reduction in air pollution, China is now planning to bring sixty new nuclear reactors online to meet the country's growing energy needs and reduce emissions. They have also increased their solar panel use and are now the number-one world leader in manufacturing photovoltaic panels.

India is far poorer than China; eight hundred million Indian citizens rely on wood and coal for cooking, and three hundred million burn kerosene lamps for light, causing tremendous pollution and health consequences. The Indian government has acknowledged the problem, but due to economic priorities and the poverty of much of the population, they consider a carbon cap unrealistic. They realize that, historically, no country has elevated its economy and standard of living without an increase of energy per capita. India has, however, recently stated they want to adhere to the to the Paris Accord. That should give us further impetus to enact this initiative and to develop safer alternative sustainable energy resources that all nations—including our own—can use. Not to do so is to contaminate breathable air for everyone.

Because our country is both the biggest economy in the world and the biggest per-capita polluter, we have a moral imperative to be the example and take leadership in reversing this harmful trend. Again, I encourage our national leaders to adhere to the Paris Accord and join the worldwide effort to clean up our environment. It would be shameful to be the only developed country not to do so.

MANAGING ABUNDANT CLEAN ENERGY

The rule of electricity usage is that the amount generated and put into the grid must equal the amount consumed. When too much electricity is put into our outdated transmission lines and power plants, they can break down and cause blackouts. During its transition from nonrenewable fossil fuels to renewable energy sources, California has occasionally had to turn off huge solar and wind farms because too much electricity was being generated for the grid to handle. In a few instances, it has also had to *pay* Nevada, Arizona, and other states to take the extra electricity. To smooth out the flow of electricity, the California Public Utility Commission has ordered the installation of large lithium batteries to store the excess electricity during times of peak production. The excess electricity is released during peak usage, when the sun isn't shining, or on windless days.

Batteries are essential for clean energy usage. The goal is to achieve fast-charging, long-life batteries that store excess energy such as in the above case. Basically, a battery is containerized stored energy. It is fair to say that a battery is like an electron piggy bank. You "charge" the bank by putting in electrons and withdraw the electrons when you need them. Batteries can store energy in different ways. For example, planners at Swan Lake in Oregon are proposing batteries that use sunlight to produce solar power during peak production—when extra electrons are available—to pump lake water to a hilltop "holding reservoir" above. At night, when the solar cells stop operating and electricity is needed, the reservoir's dams are opened, and the surging water flowing downhill turns turbines to generate electricity. This method is called *pumped-storage electricity* and is already being used by the San Diego County Water Authority and other sites in the country. This is a *hydroelectric* piggy bank.

Batteries can also store energy in the form of air or heat. Excess power generated during peak hours can be used to run an air compressor that pumps air into a large, sealed underground cavern. Then, when power is needed during off-peak production times, the encapsulated compressed air is released to turn turbine generators producing electricity. This has been termed a *giant air* type of piggy bank.

Thermal energy storage batteries store heat in large cylinders of salt. When solar production goes offline in the late afternoon, the stored heat is used to run turbines—a *hot salt* piggy bank of sorts. There are also flywheel energy storage batteries and regenerative fuel cells, among others. As more time progresses, even more innovations will arise and prove not only to be more efficient, but more economical as well.

The importance of battery technology is that many clean-renewable sources depend on the whims of wind and sun availability and are not always dependable. As mentioned, we may produce more electricity than we need during peak daylight times, but when people return home from work at night, the energy demand increases. It is important that we establish an efficient and secure national grid tied in to all these energy sources and backed up by battery supplies to balance day and night needs and distribute stored electricity in an economical, efficient manner.

There are hundreds of new ideas for energy production, from fabrics with lining that generates electron flow from the movement of your body to roads with special surface treatments that generate transferable energy from tire friction. Future car batteries will be able to be charged much faster and last longer than present ones. There is hope! We are just beginning a long quest to find new and better ways, and we will. There is abundant reward for those private enterprises that strive for innovative ways to produce and store energy; government should also provide incentives for battery technology and as mentioned, encourage garages and parking areas to offer charging stations to foster greater utilization.

This NMA initiative should also support and coordinate standards that will accelerate further development and application models that will bring efficient, long-lasting batteries to market in the near future. As more safe, clean, renewable alternatives to burning fossil fuels become available, the goal is to store as much electricity as possible to be used during peak utilization hours or in case of emergency blackouts. As a modernized national grid comes online, power can also be transferred from areas of non-peak usage to areas of peak usage. While the sun is still shining on the West Coast, producing more energy than can be consumed there, the excess electricity can be transferred over a modernized national grid throughout our country to the darkened East Coast to light the way.

In the future, homes and buildings may have their own electrical production and battery storage panels in order to maintain a constant source of electricity. In the future, perhaps everyone will have a self-sufficient standalone energy resource.

The combined application of clean energy sources and battery storage can reduce the need to burn coal or oil and supply electricity without producing toxic pollutants or additional greenhouse gases. Tax incentives and subsidies for research to development feasible types of energy storage systems might reduce tax revenues slightly, but they would save billions of dollars for electric ratepayers.

The next section on climate change stability - a present paramount crisis - must be addressed immediately. Global warming effects causing more extreme droughts and wider ranging forest fires, sea level rises and more frequent floods, catastrophic hurricanes and record storm surges are more than a threat to our future; they are all happening now and are predicted to get much worse.

CHAPTER 5

CLIMATE CHANGE STABILITY

As you read this section, consider it in terms of the coordinated, holistic way your physical body functions and the way we want the component parts of this initiative to work.

Our atmospheric climate surrounds and protects our planet and is similar to the skin that surrounds us and protects our body. Our atmosphere protects us from particles large and small, from ultraviolet rays to meteor showers, just as our skin protects us from over the thousands of species of microbes that exist on its surface. Our atmosphere and our skin also insulate us and help regulate our temperature. When our body's temperature gets too hot or too cold, it is a sign of illness. We must maintain a temperature near 98.6 degrees to remain healthy. If our planet's temperature gets too hot or too cold (like the ice age) it is also a sign of danger to our health. We and other life-forms require a safe range of environmental temperatures in order to exist.

Climatologists who have rigorously studied glacial ice core samples, fossils, and carbon-dating data know that our planet has had many extremes of hot and cold cycles. Cyclic swings are a natural phenomenon. Conditions immediately following our planet's formation 4.5 billion years ago did not permit living organisms to arise. Then, during the Cambrian period—approximately 550 million years ago—tiny organisms such as protozoa and others appeared. As environmental living conditions changed and evolved, larger and more complicated life forms appeared. Many of the life forms that once existed—such as the dinosaurs of the Jurassic period, sixty-five million years ago—are now extinct because their climate and habitat were not able to sustain them.

Living organisms need specific environmental conditions to survive. The three most important elements are breathable air, potable water, and sources of food. If the environment cannot supply one of these essential elements to any species, that species will die off. Past ice ages have killed off many species, as have periods when the temperatures were too high, resulting in extended droughts denying water to plants and animals. Each species that could not adapt became extinct.

In earth's long history, our human species has existed for only a tiny speck of time. During our time on the planet, our early ancestors foraged for edible plants, searched for water, and hunted animals for sustenance. Our numbers were few, and our hardships were many. Our survival depended on our environment to provide water, food, and compatible temperatures to support us. Fortunately, humanity has developed a remarkably high degree of adaptability, which has allowed our numbers to increase greatly. Many of us now have heating and air-conditioning to control our indoor temperatures; a large percentage of our population has plumbing and water pipeline supplies; and we have a global food chain to feed most of our species. Extreme poverty, drought, and loss of agricultural and natural food sources unfortunately deny many people the basic necessities of life, yet the majority of our species survives, and a growing portion of us thrives.

But there is a clear and present danger that larger numbers of our species may fall upon extreme hardships and may not survive due to climatic changes. There is also the smaller possibility of the total extinction of our species. If that were to happen, the span of our existence would measure only as a minuscule moment in the 4.5 billion years of earth's existence—and our planet would continue to spin on its axis without us.

In the past, the earth's environment always governed what life could exist on the planet. Today the reverse is true—humanity is now affecting the planetary environment. This new epoch is called the Anthropocene or Anthropogenic Age. "Anthropoid" means "human" in Greek, and "cene" means "new." The Jurassic age was the time of dinosaurs; the Anthropocene age has been officially designated by the International Union of Geological Sciences as the "age of the humans."

Humanity has worked to establish the best possible living conditions for itself. Other species also establish their unique habitats, but are limited to areas of the land or sea that can support their lives. Humanity's habitat is the whole planet; from deserts to rain forests, high mountain peaks to tropical islands and the Arctic. No other single species has had such power to affect the whole planet in the multitude of ways that we do. So awesome is our power that we haven't always recognized it. We are so powerful that we can literally punch a hole in our stratosphere—and we actually did that without even realizing it.

We were innocent. We didn't intend any harm. We just used aerosol sprays for our daily needs such as hairspray, deodorant, and cleaning solutions. When we realized what we had done, we banned hydro fluorocarbon (HFC) gases for spray use on a global scale and passed laws limiting it in refrigeration and air conditioning. Since then, the ozone hole has been closing, which will better protect our species from skin cancer and other maladies. Although reductions have been ongoing, the problem has not been solved, as not all nations are honoring the ban. And since HFC emissions are one thousand times more potent than carbon emissions in affecting global temperatures, the corrective measures in use need to be strongly encouraged and followed through.

On a planetary scale, humanity's massive collective actions, innocent or otherwise, have a significantly powerful effect on all living things. It is now well known what contaminants pollute our seas and air, and we can no longer claim innocence if we continue in our present ways.

There is, however, hope—hope to remedy our dilemma and provide greater benefits for all. Humanity recognized the hole in the ozone layer and has collectively made beneficial corrective changes; the world's population is better for those actions. This NMA initiative sets in motion legislative guidelines we now need to make to address today's global environmental problems. When fully enacted, it can also serve as an example for other countries. With a greater holistic awareness of our problems, and with willingness and resolve to make the necessary changes, there is hope in our present "age of humans."

Other dangers of our human activity are the consequences of our land use: our influence on ecosystems and biodiversity can lead to extinction of species. Land use may seem like an innocuous activity, and on a very small scale it is. But on a larger scale, it is something to be reckoned with. If you were to fly over New York City or San Francisco only a few hundred years ago, you would have seen only forested lands inhabited by bears, deer, and other wildlife. When you look down at those cities today, all you see are buildings, roads, homes, and a sprinkling of trees—most of which were domestically planted. You will not see deer or bears or large forests within those city areas. The forests of the past contained the ecosystems to support those wildlife creatures. On a small scale, to lose a forest the size of New York City or San Francisco may not be critical. However, when you geographically expand the size of those cities and take into consideration that *half of today's world population now lives in urban areas*, the effects of our human activity on the survivability of other species locally and worldwide become evident.

After the trees are cleared off and water is diverted, the land can no longer support the species that once existed there. Large mammals have become extinct in the past; keep in mind that we humans are large mammals. Trees shade the ground to keep it cool and help clean the air of carbon. Buildings, homes, and industry generate abundant heat: asphalt roads absorb 90 percent of the heat from the sun's rays, and cars' exhaust and engines form city "heat islands" that raise the temperature of the environment.

This doesn't mean we shouldn't build roads and buildings, but we definitely need to know what the consequences are and how to prevent the situation from getting further out of hand. Some planners, for example, are now requiring "cool" roofs and pavements that reflect the sun and absorb less heat. We all need a home to live in, a place to work, and the means to travel between the two, but there are ways to seek a balance with our living habits and not interfere with nature's ways of supporting life.

Every day, we need to eat—all 7.5 billion of us. The Midwest is the breadbasket of the United States, and when you fly over it today, you will see large circles of agricultural fields. The circles are there because the most efficient way to irrigate those fields is with one centered sprinkling pipe turning on its radius. The trees and the other natural flora and fauna that once flourished there are now vastly diminished or nonexistent. Forests and large land areas around the globe have been cleared for humanity's agricultural, commercial, and industrial needs—half of all the trees that once existed on the planet are now gone. States such as Texas, Montana, and Wyoming have cleared the land for cattle to graze on, and the ecosystems and migratory paths supporting each states' indigenous wildlife have been severely compromised. We do not intentionally want to harm nature in order to maintain abundant food supplies, but that is a consequence of our actions. Imbalanced land use has consequences that can come back to bite us, and we must work smarter so that we can benefit and nature will not be harmed.

The near extinction of our nation's most iconic symbol—the American bald eagle—was a particularly harsh lesson. Many years ago, in order to eradicate insects that were harming crop production, we used the pesticide DDT. It killed lots of insects, and we had better crops—for a while. But as time went by, we eventually became aware that it was also killing a lot of other life that we held very dear and needed to sustain the ecosystems that supported our lives. DDT permeated the soil and the foods we grew in it. Countless species were harmed, and many began dying off—the American bald eagle was one of them. DDT interfered with their production of eggshells, making them so thin that they often broke during incubation. Our national symbol of strength was becoming extinct. Again, we were innocent. We hadn't intended to kill off our American eagle. The use of DDT was banned, and the hunting of eagles became a crime. Today the American eagle has made a comeback because our awareness compelled us to take the steps necessary to correct our mistakes.

Our climate, for better or worse, affects trees, birds, fish, and all the wildlife in our ecosystems. All ecosystems affect our environment. In this age of humans, the human ecosystem that we have created is affecting all life on our planet, especially ourselves. As we have grown through time, we have achieved amazing accomplishments; we have also made many mistakes because of our ignorance, but with awareness we have corrected many of those mistakes. Hopefully, the contents of this proposal will compel us to correct our current mistakes. Going forward, we must keep a simple truth in mind: *we need nature to survive—nature does not need us.*

Today we face a grave threat to our way of life and perhaps our very existence: global warming. It has become a controversial issue that has raised many crucial questions: Did humanity cause it? Is it just a natural occurrence? Can anything be done about it? Is it just a hoax? Is it even really happening?

The primary responsibility of the United States Department of Defense is to protect us and ensure our safety. In 2014, the Pentagon issued a chilling report titled, "The Climate Change Adaptation Road Map." It stated that "rising global temperatures, changing precipitation patterns, climbing sea levels, and more extreme weather events will intensify the challenges of global instability, hunger, poverty, and conflict. They will likely lead to food and water shortages, pandemic disease, disputes over refugees and resources, and destruction by natural disasters in regions across the globe."

The United States Navy has also observed signs of increasing global warming in the form of rising sea levels due to the rapid acceleration of Arctic ice melt. They have been planning to build canals to move vulnerable ports further inland so that their vessels will not become unmoored or damaged when high tides and hurricanes occur.

These actions are mentioned because they are clearly not politically motivated. They have been proposed because the Department of Defense must work strategically with all the data at its disposal to protect our safety. In their opinion, global warming is really happening. It is not a hoax.

Exxon, the world's largest oil and gas company, has long known about global warming but suppressed their research findings until recently. At a 2017 summer shareholders meeting, angry demands were made to the board of directors, asking about their future policy. Those shareholders, with hundreds of millions of dollars in Exxon stock, feared diminishing returns on their investment if corrective action was not taken. They were well aware of the growing global shift away from fossil fuels. It is notable that instead of ads for gasoline fuel, Exxon TV commercials now show pictures of green algae growing as they strive to develop new clean energy sources.

Surprisingly, even Saudi Arabia, the world's largest exporter of oil, is seeking to reduce its reliance on petrodollars as it foresees demand and price sinking lower in the future. They plan to develop other sources of revenue such as mining and tourism. There is constant growing acknowledgment of global warming and the shift away from oil.

Two reliable scientific instruments that everyone is familiar with can easily be used to ascertain the extent of global warming changes—a thermometer and a ruler. Every day and everywhere around the world, the temperature of our atmosphere is measured. Thermometers also measure ocean temperatures. The recorded readings speak for themselves. It is undeniable that our global temperatures have been rising: in very recent years, we have had the hottest annual temperature readings ever recorded—each year hotter than the last, and the year 2016 the hottest yet. As this book goes to press, during the 2016-17 weather seasons we have experienced record rains, record heat, record floods, record fires, and tornadoes—all a result of global warming. Unfortunately, these dangers are expected to increase and intensify.

There are also surprising consequences that are occurring that most people haven't heard about before. As the temperature gets hotter, the gas molecules that make up air spread further apart, causing the air to thin. Less dense air reduces lift to aircraft wings on takeoff. In June of 2017, American Airlines had to cancel sixty flights in Phoenix, Arizona when temperatures reached 119 degrees. The planes' wing designs do not allow operation at temperatures higher than 117.8 degrees. With more expected future heat waves, expect more future flight cancellations. A lot of summer vacation plans will be disrupted, and airlines will lose revenue.

What alarms many climatologists most is not the fact that the temperatures have been increasing in the ocean, air, and land, but that *the rate of increase is rapidly accelerating.* Recorded temperatures around the world verify that global warming is all too real and that it is occurring at an accelerated rate.

Rulers measure the height of rising sea levels, another consequence of global warming. Satellite imagery measures the melting of land-based glacial ice—and tell us that we have lost over 70 percent of it in a startlingly short time over the last few years.. The melted water goes into our seas, and the sea level raises. Residents of Miami know this only too well: when there are high tides, inflowing seawater from drainage pipes floods the streets, even when the sun is shining and there is no rain. In December of 2016, an octopus was found in a parking lot.

The recent September 2017 catastrophe of hurricanes Harvey, Irma and Maria that brought devastation to Houston, Texas and other Gulf states, Puerto Rico, the Caribbean islands and in Florida was extraordinary due to their immense intensity. The increase in water temperatures caused the hurricane to soak up more moisture, and as it approached land, record winds and rains fell (over 1 trillion gallons in Houston) accompanied by devastating surges of seawater pushed by the forceful winds. Hurricane Harvey that devastated Houston is another prime example of global warming consequences. Those two storms have left an indelible imprint in our American psyche of people walking the streets of their hometowns in waist deep water searching for shelter. Many lost everything they owned. Millions of people lost electricity, unimagined amounts of storm surge water inundated the land and hundreds of thousands of people had no fresh water to drink.

There is also a great need to improve our water systems that supply fresh water and adequate drainage systems in the instances of flooding. Present systems to help mitigate flooding from catastrophic rainfalls need immediate updating and were not noted in the infrastructure improvements section of this initiative, but are mentioned here in this section because we can readily see the countless hardships of lost homes and businesses due to global warming and record rainfalls. This is another illustration why all aspects of this initiative are interrelated and need to be coordinated in a holistic fashion to ensure the safety and health of our country's population.

A far more alarming development is that small, sea-level islands are actually in the process of disappearing from the surface of our planet because of sea levels rising above their lands. Citizens of some island nations are literally losing their countries and becoming refugees seeking a new homeland. Unlike most refugees, however, they never will be able to return home. In 1992, President Maumoon Abdul Gayoom of the Maldives plaintively addressed the United Nations' Earth Summit. He spoke with great concern for his tiny island in the Indian Ocean and said, "I stand before you as a representative of an endangered people. We are told that as a result of global warming and sea level rise, my country, the Maldives, may sometime during the next century, disappear from the face of the earth." Coastal cities throughout the world may face the same fate if nothing changes and the trends of global warming continue.

Rulers not only measure how high sea levels have risen, they also measure how far down the land has sunk. In addition to a rise in sea levels, global warming has also brought about severe droughts that have caused the earth in those areas to lose water through evaporation, depletion of underground aquifers due to the increased need to irrigate crops, and lack of rain. The weight of the soil causes the earth to sink in on itself, becoming compressed due to lack of moisture. This compression is lasting, because when rains do come, the soil is packed too hard to absorb them. In parts of California, land surface levels have sunk six feet or more, causing small bridges over streams to drop to the water level.

Some people will say that global warming is just a hoax. They will deny it is even really happening. If an exhausted polar bear could talk after catching its breath from swimming miles looking for an ice floe to climb on and rest before it drowns, it would definitely confirm that there is no doubt global warming is real. A survey of international scientists revealed that an overwhelming 97 percent confirmed that global warming is a fact. A mere 3 percent would not agree. What do you think?

Some people may legitimately ask if human activity is actually causing global warming or if it's just a natural occurrence. As mentioned, the earth has had many natural cycles of hot and cold shifts, and there are too many unknowns to be absolutely certain that humanity *alone* is 100 percent responsible, although many studies has shown that human activity is the cause. What is known is that human activities are definitely contributing to global warming and that the rate of global warming is accelerating. There are no Democratic or Republican or religious thermometers or rulers to sway their readings. It is dangerous folly to deny that global warming is not only occurring but is rapidly increasing. It is also dangerous folly to ignore its disastrous consequences.

In addition to the simple basic measuring instruments of a thermometer and a ruler, there are also many sophisticated satellites collecting data including land surfaces mentioned that have sunk, carbon levels in the atmosphere, and weather pattern shifts. The Trump administration, to save money, has stopped funding the operations of these vital satellites, blinding us to what is actually happening to our environment. I beseech the administration to turn the lights back on so we do not have to dwell in the darkness of ignorance. The cost of a battery for a smoke detector is a small price to pay to be alerted to danger of fire.

But can anything actually be done to stabilize climate change?

Yes! A lot can be done, and this initiative is one of the things that will thrust us forward toward our goal of reducing the rate of global warming. Reducing carbon emissions and using renewable energy sources that are sustainable and nonpolluting are huge factors in achieving that goal.

Our current activities produce greenhouse gases that are adding to the acceleration of global warming. As sunlight passes through the glass panes of a greenhouse, it raises the temperature of the space and the objects inside. Those objects absorb the solar heat and then radiate extra heat to normalize the temperature uniformly within the enclosed area. That extra radiant heat is not in the form of sunlight (photons and light waves) and does not pass back through the glass panes; instead, it remains trapped and increases the temperature within the greenhouse. When carbon-based fuels burn, they release carbon particles into our atmosphere and form a "carbon blanket" around our planet. The "blanket" allows sunlight through to heat our planet's land surface, atmosphere, and oceans, and the land and water radiate heat back into our atmosphere. But just like an insulating blanket keeps you warm at night by trapping the heat your body radiates, our current carbon blanket contains this radiant heat and does not let it escape back into space.

Science tells us that since the industrial revolution, the increased burning of carbon-based fuels has resulted in an ongoing acceleration and accumulation of carbon added to our atmosphere—it's like adding extra blankets even though you're already warm enough; it just gets hotter and more uncomfortable. The carbon added to our atmosphere unfortunately stays there for hundreds of years, and our thickening carbon blanket is creating an ever more uncomfortable environment for all the ecosystems on our planet. This hothouse effect has already made conditions unlivable for an expanding list of species.

There is no doubt that the temperature of our planet is rising and that weather patterns are shifting. Some people say it's the earth's natural cycle, others say that humanity is responsible, and still others think it doesn't matter, because nothing can be done about it anyway.

Does it really matter?

Consider this analogy: if you heat a pot of water on the stove, bring it to a steaming boil, and then hold your hand six inches above it, your hand will get very hot in a short time and you would quickly pull it away. If you turn off the burner, wait one minute, and *then* put your hand six inches over the pot, you would feel warmth but not need to pull your hand away. That's because air temperatures can heat and cool quickly.

You certainly wouldn't think of putting your hand into the pot of water itself, however, even if the boiling steam had stopped a minute ago. You know that boiling hot water takes quite a bit longer to cool down to room temperature. That's because water has a significantly greater density of molecules and retains heat for far longer periods than the air.

Our atmospheric weather patterns fluctuate over short times. Think of summer heat and winter cold: many regions may experience a temperature shift of nearly a hundred degrees over the course of a year, from broiling sticky days at the peak of summer to freezing nights in the depth of winter. Air temperature is a short-term consequence of global warming compared to the long-term consequence of our oceans getting hotter. Our oceans absorb much of the excess heat being retained in our atmosphere, and like the boiling pot of water, they will take a much longer time to cool. Rising ocean temperatures add to glacial melting and a rise in sea levels, as well as to shifts in weather patterns that produce record floods, droughts, hurricanes, tornados, desertification, and a deadly increase of wildfires.

Global warming increases the rate of glacial melting, which becomes partially self-propelled by water pooling on top of the ice. The darker-blue water absorbs heat from the sun, rather than reflecting it like the white ice. That causes further ice melts, producing more water to pool, which absorbs more heat, and on and on. Additionally, as ocean temperatures increase near a glacier, its rate of calving (when huge chunks of the glacier split off and fall into the ocean) increases until it eventually melts. And all of this glacial land ice goes into our oceans, raising sea levels and causing greater coastal flooding.

Let's say that humanity *didn't* cause the problem of global warming. We still know that the planet's land and ocean temperatures have measurably been on the upswing. We know that water boils at 212 degrees Fahrenheit. We also know that whether or not we caused the problem, our present use of fossil fuels for energy definitely adds to it. If the temperature of the water in the pot on the stove is 210 degrees, it will not boil and steam; if you add only two degrees more, you will bring the water to a steaming boil. Those two degrees are a significant tipping point.

Oceans are not going to come to a boil, but there are indications that we may be reaching a point of no return affecting sea life in the bodies of water that cover three quarters of our planet's surface—and we don't know exactly what that tipping point is. Ocean currents constantly blend and mix their own seawater "smoothie," stirring pollutants and warmer temperatures throughout. This has been causing massive coral die-offs. Coral is not a plant but a living animal, and some coral colonies have taken centuries to grow. Coral in locations as far apart as the Caribbean, Key West, the Great Barrier Reef in Australia, and Hawaii has been affected and turned to skeleton white. The coral of the Great Barrier Reef is the largest living organism on earth, of which 70 percent has died off. Coral allows smaller fish to hide from predators and mate in secure areas, and the algae that grows over the coral (giving it its color) provides food for them to eat. Coral barrier reefs also protect shorelines from erosion.

Fish are migrating further north to more habitable cooler water, which is leading to unexpected consequences. There has been a sharp increase in predator shark sightings off Monterey, California. California has also seen a huge die-off of young seals due to undernourishment because the warming temperatures have caused increased acidity—the warmer water absorbs atmospheric carbon and forms carbonic acid. That in turn has caused an imbalance of the aquatic food chain. The algae migrate north to cooler water, followed by the aquatic life and smaller fish that feed on them, leaving inadequate food for the seals. We know that ice floes for polar bears to rest on after swimming in the frigid sea have diminished, and that the bears have also been dying off. Most alarming is that our Arctic ice cap has been melting like an ice cube under the summer sun. In 2015, Greenland lost 70 percent of its ice coverings, after it had lost 36 percent the year before. Asia's highest temperature ever was recorded in Kuwait: 129.2 degrees. Death Valley, California cooked hotter than ever in July 2017, breaking a one hundred-year-old record for the hottest month. Portland, Oregon, with average summer temperatures normally peaking in the seventies, suffered many days in the hundreds and an all-time record of 107 degrees. Due to heat expansion of train rails, Portland's light rail system was forced to slow its operating speed to thirty-five miles per hour, causing many delays

This aspect of global warming is noted because it is another unexpected consequence illustrating the urgency that we must do all within our power to avoid adding any more heat and to reduce the heat we do produce as much as possible. Once the oceans reach that tipping point...well, we just cannot add those few extra degrees of heat, or we will be cooking ourselves.

Another critical point of concern is the release of methane into our atmosphere. Methane is a constituent of the natural gas used for fuel. Oil drilling, leaky gas pipes, and manufacturing account for 25 percent of artificial greenhouse gases. Methane, labeled a "super pollutant," is eighty-four times more potent as a pollutant than carbon dioxide. Capping off oil wells and regulating pipeline leakage will reduce manmade greenhouse gases, and the saved methane can be used to generate electricity. This has been resisted by the oil and drilling industry.

Naturally decomposing organic material from plants and animals also produces methane. In our recent age of humans, global warming has caused a rapid melting of the Arctic permafrost and tundra. Tundra is formed from shrubs, lichens, and mosses, which release methane as they decompose. The age-old semi-frozen tundra belt is 4.5 million square miles across northern Russia and Canada and contains countless tons of potential methane gas.

Any amount of methane released, however, will add to today's accumulated greenhouse gases, and we are approaching another drastic tipping point. With increased global warming, as the permafrost melts, megatons of vegetation will begin to decay in the mushy wetlands and release methane. The more methane is released, the faster the acceleration of global warming, which will speed the ongoing melting of the frozen tundra, which will raise global temperatures, and on and on...

No one yet knows what the full consequences will be, but a self-perpetuating cycle has been initiated. Once the tundra gases escape, we cannot put that super-pollutant genie back in the bottle. This is another reason to put the brakes on global warming now!

At the risk of being repetitious, I feel it important to mention again that on a per capita basis, our country is in fact the number-one polluter in the world. We also enjoy the benefits of the number one-economy and the largest GDP in recorded history. As such, we have the moral responsibility to take the lead in reversing our dubious role and becoming the number-one example of a clean energy nation. Again, I encourage our national leaders to remain in the Paris accord and to join the worldwide effort to help stabilize global warming. Failure to do so hurts us all. The United States needs to align with the hopes and desires of the rest of the world to preserve our environment and health.

Those who oppose climate protections thinking they threaten our economy do not often see the whole picture. From 2009 to 2015, greenhouse gases in the United States were reduced by 10 percent, and our economy grew over 15 percent. We can definitely achieve cleaner air, help stabilize climate change, and create prosperity at the same time. In fact, cleaner energy is becoming cheaper to use than toxic fossil fuels. This choice should not be an either-or decision. That is why this initiative emphasizes the concept of a win-win strategy with mutual benefit for all.

There will always be interests opposed to this National Modernization Act for self-serving political or monetary reasons, but in the final analysis, a sustainable environment is the ultimate basic human right. Let's not go backward and play the blame game. Instead, let's move forward in establishing a clean environment and a transportation system fueled by safe, renewable resources with zero tailpipe emissions. It is a commonsense goal for the common good.

There was no mention of global warming in the prior section of this initiative that addressed "toxic versus clean" energy sources. The reason as stated is that removing highly toxic substances and smog from the air we breathe is an obvious critical priority on its own. When the devastating consequences of global warming are added to the equation, the combined weight dramatically tips the scale in overwhelming favor of the goals of this initiative.

Given today's political climate, it should be remembered that it was Richard Nixon, a conservative Republican president, who signed the Clean Air Act into law. It's hard to fathom that anyone would have to think about whether it is a good idea to strive for clean air. Who would rationally vote for a Bad Air Act? Shouldn't our environment have the cleanest air possible?

The US Navy's road map of how to prepare for global warming laid out a path to ensure that they will be ready and able to fulfill their mission of protecting our country. This initiative is a road map for Congress to fulfill its mission and lead the way to protecting our welfare.

A leaked summer 2017 draft prepared by thirteen government agencies—part of the National Climate Assessment report mandated by Congress to be published every four years—revealed that *human caused global warming is really happening.* Temperatures are higher and rising faster than in the last seventeen hundred years. They predict more record temperatures, higher mean sea level rises, greater sea ice melts, and heavier record rainfalls. Those in the know, know this cannot go on unchecked.

What needs to be done now? To accomplish the goals of this initiative will take a strong and unified political will. This need not be a challenge to incumbents unless money interests thwart its implementation. This is to be expected, but vast numbers of people and national organizations already support many aspects of this initiative. Now is the time to coalesce together as a unified, overwhelming, powerful voice to make those vital changes a reality.

As an individual, your feelings and opinions are important; unified with hundreds of thousands of like hearts and minds like yours, our collective feelings become a potent force for change. Make your voice loud and clear to all within your sphere of influence. Contact your state representatives to submit and support NMA bills in the house and senate, preferably as bipartisan submissions. That is your power to use: please use it. (Ways to do so appear on pages 80-81.) When our leaders and lawmakers in government work together in a spirit of cooperation, our country—and the world—will be better for it.

Don't be distracted by the argument about whether or not human activity is the cause of global warming—it doesn't matter now. What matters is that global warming is a fact and that we must do all we can to stabilize and reverse it.

With this initiative, the seeds of beneficial change will be cast to Congress. We the people must encourage those seeds to blossom so we can all continue to enjoy the bountiful living conditions of our planet. We are now in a position to be the caretakers of our planet, and we need to do so—or our planet will not be able to take care of us.

We can make the "Age of Humans" an age to be proud of. We can create a healthier, cleaner, and safer world, and at the same time we can also create greater prosperity. Let's go all in! Let's do it!

The next section addresses our most precious form of energy— our people.

CHAPTER 6

JOBS—A REDEPLOYMENT, EMPLOYMENT, AND TRAINING PROGRAM

O f all the energy sources available to power our nation, the most precious energy we have is *human energy*—ourselves.

We are a collection of families who share a common land. A family is made up of many individuals, often with viewpoints that sometimes conflict—yet, they still make a family. Each family member possesses unique traits and talents that define his or her character. Collections of families make up a community, collections of communities make up a county, counties form a state, and all of our states combined form the United States of America. "E Pluribus Unum - Out of Many, One"

Like people, each family, community, and state has unique traits and talents that form its character. Those different collective traits and talents have blended and worked together over more than two hundred years to make America the nation it is today. Despite past errors, despite instances of intermittent territorial and political animosity, America is still looked upon by the majority of the world as a place of freedom and opportunity that allows individuals to succeed.

For the poor and oppressed in the world, our country is looked upon as a place of hope. Many of today's America's citizens have come to the United States from around the world and succeeded here. They have attained success in areas across the board by striving for achievement and using their unique traits and talents in the best way they could under whatever circumstances prevailed at the time. Our collective accomplishments have contributed to making America the most successful nation in the world. Blending and using our differences successfully has been the winning formula.

But now many Americans feel far differently from those outside of our country who view America as a place of freedom, hope, and opportunity. Those Americans' feelings of anger, resentment, distrust, powerlessness, frustration, and alienation have created a climate of polarization that has been festering over the recent years.

Other nations throughout the world have not been immune to the global phenomena of political conflict and emotional strife. The polarizing turmoil is pandemic. One underlying force behind this stressful turmoil is the accelerating rate of change in all levels of our lives. Many people perceive this as a time of uncertainty and perhaps danger, but history tells us that marvelous advancements and greater prosperity often follow times of great change. That is why today, in the midst of what seems like chaos, we can establish a program of great opportunity and a renewed hope.

Hope and the opportunity to succeed have always been the great energizing forces propelling America. When hope is lost, people will often just stop trying or lash out in their anger and frustration. The truth is that there are many ways to better our circumstances, renew our hope, and maintain a sense of unity and purpose. It's not a lost cause; it is within our present reach. In this world of accelerating change and turmoil, this is a pivotal time in which we can create success out of our present struggles by utilizing our precious human energy in more creative and beneficial ways.

That is why a means to revitalize and reapply our human energy potential may be the most significant part of this National Modernization Act; we must once again lend our unique traits and talents as individuals, communities, and states to a common goal of improving our country on a physical, emotional, and spiritual level. It is within our present ability to create a peaceful and prosperous way of life for the American family. This initiative is not only intended to modernize our infrastructure, it is also intended to modernize the deployment of our workforce.

As the old saying has it, give a person a fish, and he can eat for a day; *teach* a person to fish, and she will be able to feed herself for life. That is the essence of this redeployment, employment, and training proposal, to provide a means for people to qualify for better paying and meaningful work—and to keep working.

In order to achieve that goal, the overwhelming majority of the people in this, the richest country in the world, must feel that they are able to earn a truly livable wage and support their families. In doing so, they will also be better able to support their communities. Each state will do much better, and America will do far better as a whole. It has always been the energy of our hearts and souls that has sustained America. This initiative is intended to harness that magnificent force to reignite our spirit. With our individual freedoms, coupled with our willingness to work together, America has historically created innovative new ideas and better ways of doing things to meet the challenges at hand. Today we have the opportunity to meet those challenges.

Redeployment, employment, and training (RET), together, provide one such way. Currently there are numerous governmental employment resources listing job opportunities in many fields. Existing data such as those maintained by the United States Bureau of Labor Statistics and others can provide templates catered to specific employment needs for modernizing our infrastructure and our transition to clean energy.

Mobilizing our workforce will not be unlike mobilizing our voluntary armed forces. New recruits will receive basic training in a variety of skills to be deployed in their local vicinity and other areas where needed if they choose to relocate. The soldiers who serve in combat are only one part of our armed forces. It takes all kinds of skilled workers to run and maintain armies: carpenters, engineers, laborers, computer operators, accountants, truck drivers, and chefs, to name a few. As the landscape of our defense needs changes, personnel are *retrained* and *redeployed* to serve those needs or are shifted from one sector of service to another, where their present skills can better be utilized. They are not laid off and forced into unemployment. The armed forces continually reevaluate present and future anticipated needs for service personnel and adapt accordingly. It is imperative for them to do so in order to fulfill their mission.

The same kind of strategic thinking is necessary to maximize employment and utilize our civilian workforce in the most effective way possible. It is our civilian workforce that supplies the funding needed to keep our armed forces at the ready, and our workforce itself needs to be mobilized to stay competitive and productive in the highly competitive global economy. Redeployment, employment, and training differ from extant programs in that they provide the means to meet those obligations specifically for the implementation for this initiative.

This three-pronged proposal can be simply defined as follows:

Redeployment applies to people who have work experience and skills but who are now unemployed and seeking suitable work, as well as to those who are presently employed but need to move to a new area or seek a better job commensurate with their skills and income needs.

Employment applies to people without work experience who may possess needed skills or have been schooled or trained in specific areas and are ready to enter the workforce and need placement.

Training encompasses two components. *Basic training* is for people without prior skills. They will be trained in skills needed both in the present and in the projected job market, matched with their natural traits and talents. *Specialty training* is for people with prior skills who seek new modes of work that will be needed in the future with ensured placement.

A recruitment campaign for this initiative, similar to the ways in which the armed forces encourage enlistments to meet their needs, is essential. Public service announcements and social media resources, among others, should be utilized. The target audience would include high schools, colleges, and state and local employment agencies. When individuals join the RET program, an analysis of their acquired skills and natural aptitudes will be matched with a national database bank and cross-referenced with employers' current and projected job needs. Successful businesses, especially large companies, plan for their business needs years in advance. Presently there is a dearth of skilled people to fulfill employers' needs. Those businesses would greatly benefit by having a source of employees trained in those needed skills.

Trainees will greatly benefit from their participation, knowing that they have a high probability of securing a job after the program is completed. This is a win-win; it ensures smoother transitions for employees and continued productivity for companies. Tax incentives and other inducements can be made for private companies that pay—partially or in full—for the training. In other cases, training costs specifically for the NMA may be underwritten by this initiative. The goal is to have full employment for those who want to work and simultaneously increase our country's productivity. The NMA *national database bank* specifically modeled for this initiative would be an extension of the *Occupational Outlook Handbook* maintained by the Bureau of Labor Statistics. It will be programmed to include the likelihood of procuring a specific job, its realistic range of salary, and a brief outline of the training needed, including the time and any costs involved. This will offer those lost in the unemployment swamp hope for the future. It will offer an opportunity to make America a true land of opportunity for all.

Creating a national database bank for this initiative is absolutely within our reach. In the 1950s, Jay W. Forrester, a professor at the Massachusetts Institute of Technology developed the field of system dynamics modeling in order to help management comprehend the long-term consequences of employee hiring, inventory, market needs, and other crucial factors by using computer simulations. The program incorporated information from social and physical systems, the economy, food, pollution, population, and natural resources. System dynamics has been proven so successful over the decades that it is now used in sciences such as biology, chemistry, engineering, astrophysics, and climate studies. This modeling program can readily manage a national database bank for this initiative and for the mutual benefit of employers and employees on a national level.

To better understand the scope of the RET program, three questions need to be considered: Where have the jobs gone? Where are the jobs today? Where will the jobs be tomorrow? The answer to all three questions depends on an analysis of basic employment *trends*.

Employment Trends

In the 1950s forty percent of households had no phone, and those that did shared their phone lines with a number of other households. Conversations were supposed to be limited to five minutes so that other party-line households could use the line, and there was no privacy because another household could pick up the phone and listen in on the conversation. I often picked up the phone and started to dial when I heard someone talking and had to hang up quickly. Only a loose self-monitoring honor system allowed others to share the same limited wire network. Making a call at that time entailed entering the number on a slow, ten-hole rotary dial. There were no mobile phones, and you had to limit your movement when talking on the leash-length of the telephone cord.

Whenever someone wanted to place a call in those days, a telephone operator had to manually plug in a connecting wire on a switchboard. As switchboard automation evolved, however, human operators were no longer necessary. Today there are over two billion wireless cell phones worldwide. Billions of phone calls are made every day with no human operator. Automation has replaced those jobs, yet more people are employed in the telecommunication field than ever before.

Phones now provide for more than the means to have a conversation with someone else—they are a source of information, offering access to more resources than thousands of libraries. Smart phones can help us find a movie theater and tell us the film's starting time, inform us of the weather, or recommend a new restaurant based on our past eating experiences—and make a reservation for us. The ways in which our phones make life easier and more efficient are countless. The phone and its history provide an example of how the *trend* has been for telecommunications to change, evolve, and create new and better functions that benefit society for less cost. In 1950 a long-distance call cost about ten cents a minute—about a dollar a minute adjusted for inflation. After a base monthly fee, the same phone call today can cost less than a penny a minute—and many cell phone users have free unlimited calling.

The mythical Atlas held the world on his shoulders; modern people hold the information of the world in the palms of their hands. Your Smartphone's navigation can pinpoint your location and direct you to a destination you have never been to, yet many people cannot locate a suitable job. Many sectors in the local workplace are now competing in the global marketplace and have not been able to adapt to the trends of that changing market.

Finding oneself unemployed after previously providing an honest living for one's household is not only a depressing situation and an economic hardship, it often results in a personal feeling of hopelessness and loss of self-worth. Many unemployed people are angry and feel dejected or have fallen prey to addictive drugs, drinking, or crime. Some, in their deepest despair, have committed suicide. When many Americans lose their spirit, our spirit as a whole is diminished, as is our success.

Where have the jobs gone? There was a time when jobs in the service and manufacturing sectors were mostly filled within our country. Workers often stayed employed at the same company until they retired and received a pension. They were able to rely on a steady salary and retirement benefits. If you had a problem with a product you had bought or a service you were getting, you called the company and spoke to an in-house service representative who tried to remedy it. As time progressed, however, these calls were answered by representatives outside the country, in places as far away as India. Even though communication was difficult due to language differences, companies continued to expand their offshore hiring due to its much lower costs. American service representatives lost their jobs to cheaper labor so the companies could make a greater profit.

This scenario did not stop there. As more time progressed, Indian service representatives started to lose their own jobs as a cheaper labor market shifted to the Philippines and then to Vietnam and other developing countries. It is a double-edged sword in that people lose jobs due to cheaper offshore labor in manufacturing and services, but consumers pay less for those services and goods. People want to pay the lowest price possible for a product and are frequently unconcerned about where the product is made as long as the quality remains the same. Manufacturers and service companies want to pay the lowest price for labor and materials so they can stay competitive and make a profit. The *trend* is that the jobs go to the lowest-paid labor force to make the greatest profit, and that consumers will buy the best product they can for the lowest price possible. This has been the ongoing trend, and for the foreseeable future, this trend will continue.

As noted above, automation replaced phone operators a long time ago. In today's manufacturing world, employers that produce manufactured goods have a very obvious choice in ways to increase their profits by further lowering their labor costs. Imagine for a moment that you owned a company that employed a thousand people. If a representative of a labor-supply company came to you with the following offer, what would you do?

The representative tells you that for an initial signing fee, he can get you workers willing to do tedious, sometimes dangerous, repetitive, and precise work with no vacation time necessary, no sick leave required, no need for a human resources department to monitor working conditions, and—guaranteed—no complaints. And seven hundred of your usual one thousand weekly payroll checks will be eliminated.

What would you do? Even though it might sadden you to let go of longtime employees who have been loyal and productive, you're now competing in the global marketplace, where other businesses are selling your product for almost less money than it costs you to produce it. If your business were on the line between succeeding or failing, you would probably accept the offer. Of course, that labor supply company's "workers" are more properly called "robots," and the initial "signing bonus" is the cost of purchase.

Unfortunately, many manufacturers who have left the United States and subsequently returned to restart production have not rehired the old assembly line workers at a good living wage; instead, they have replaced those workers with robots overseen by a handful of technical people looking at their computer screens and only a handful of maintenance people to do on-site repairs. This has been a tragic blow to traditional American manufacturing workers and their families, and the damage isn't limited to the manufacturing sector. Early types of robot bartenders and coffee baristas are coming online, as well as robots that pick strawberries and grapes.

Where have the jobs gone? Many human jobs that can be done by robots have already disappeared (the automobile assembly line), and this job loss is likely to continue. That is the nature of today's global market trend. Because labor is still cheaper overseas, in many cases it is more profitable for American manufactures to have their product produced overseas and then brought back to the states for sale, resulting in greater unemployment in America's manufacturing sector.

If you have a cell phone or TV set, chances are that it was *not* manufactured in the United States. And even though your TV or phone was made in another country with cheaper labor costs, robots there did much of the assembly. No country is immune to the changing global market's tragic side effect of displacing workers. There was a time when all telephones and all TV sets were made in the United States, but those factories are gone, and so are all the jobs they provided. So how is a factory worker supposed to keep up with the global marketplace of cheaper offshore labor—and against robots? Workers cannot compete unless they learn additional skills to adapt to the needs and trends of the marketplace and unless they have help and guidance in matching their skills with the future needs of employers. That's why the redeployment, employment, and training program is necessary and has to be strategic and nimble: it must train workers to adjust to the world's anticipated constantly changing trends.

Where are the jobs today? The jobs today are in a state of transition. In fact, surveys have shown that most young people don't intend to be working at the same job or place for more than five years, and many for much less time. It has been harder for older workers to adjust to the changing trends and find work to meet their income needs. They too will benefit greatly from the redeployment, employment, and training program. Remember, an integral part of this program is job placement, which is the role of the redeployment feature.

Where will the jobs be tomorrow? With the full enactment of this National Modernization Act, there will be an abundance of good jobs available. A small army of construction workers will be needed to repair and build roads, bridges, and tunnels, to establish an updated national electric grid, and to develop and implement renewable clean energy sources. For every combat soldier on the front line, there is a backup army of other personnel in both the armed forces and the civilian sector that is necessary to provide all the facilities and supplies the soldier on the frontline needs. The same is true for the hardhat worker in the field, who also needs other workers to transport the goods, food preparers to make meals, clothing suppliers, engineers, accountants, computer programmers, and a myriad of additional occupations.

Hundreds of thousands of good paying jobs will be needed due both to the anticipated trends related to this NMA and to additional work openings not directly related to it. For example, one major obstacle to successfully repairing and updating our infrastructure is that there aren't enough skilled workers presently available. Incredibly, there have even been discussions of bringing in foreign workers to do the job. That is why the NMA is intended to operate in a holistic manner to simultaneously ensure the successful completion of infrastructure projects and establish a qualified labor force employing Americans in need of work. Implementation of the redeployment, employment, and training program will also satisfy industries' needs by training workers in the skills that are needed and then employing those people. It is a win-win for business and labor.

For a demonstration of how the program might work, look at the experience of eighteen to twenty-five-year-olds in the job market. Once these young adults have earned a high-school diploma, they may choose to go on to college if they have the money available, or they may choose to go directly into the job market. At this time, jobs for young people without experience or training usually occupy the lowest pay-scale, without many prospects for future improvement. However, young people who have gone on to college and taken on a burdensome amount of student loan debt may also not be able to find a job.

In both cases, the national employment databank would offer job applicants a variety of occupations that are currently hiring or—based on projected trends—will be hiring in the very near future. Employers may be offered certain tax incentives to fund training programs for specific skills they require to produce their specific goods and services. The very low cost of training will pale compared to the high tuition costs of college. Other supplemental funding could include payment or partial payment from applicants, depending on their income and with the option to defer payment until they are working and can deduct a small percentage annually from their salaries. Others in poor neighborhoods could receive full underwriting from government funds. The goal is to have qualified people available for jobs needed in the future so that employees and businesses can both benefit. Community colleges can offer financial aid through Pell grants and give college credits for courses in training with certification credentials in partnership with specific industries. This is a win-win strategy.

These ideas have been considered before. The Obama administration introduced the Educational Quality through Innovative Partnership (EQUIP) program, in which colleges worked with training providers allowing federal aid, grants, and loans, but only eight states were involved. R. Alexander Acosta, the current secretary of labor, under the Trump administration has recently announced an "apprenticeship" program, although details have not been released as of this writing. Secretary Acosta has stated that although less than 1 percent of workers have participated in apprenticeship programs, 90 percent of those who did had jobs waiting, with an average salary of about $60,000 a year. Rolling these elements of EQUIP and the proposed apprenticeship programs together to blend with and enhance the redeployment, employ-ment, and training program specifically designed for the NMA would be ideal.

Training and apprenticeship programs working in tandem with high schools and colleges will provide a skilled workforce to meet our future needs for jobs and business productivity. Many skills valuable to employers can be taught during the high-school years, or even earlier. When training people for skills, it's important to note that higher math and advanced English composition, which are undoubtedly valuable, are not the most important skills—or even necessary skills—in certain fields of work. Think for a mo-ment: can you remember the last time you calculated the sine or cosine of a triangle or used complicated algebraic formulas? Most of us would admit that we haven't done so since high school. This is not to say that algebra or trigonometry are not valuable tools, but the current system leaves a young person with a poor aptitude for some types of higher math with few options: many people have been prevented from graduating in the first place because they could not master trigonometry.

Lack of a high-school diploma can consign a person to a life-time of poverty, of requiring public assistance rather than contrib-uting to the public good. Skills training programs in high school would give students more incentive not to drop out, offering reas-surance that they would be able to get a job and start to make a living for themselves after graduation. Depending on their needs, students could get a *vocational* high-school diploma—the curricu-lum could be set up so higher math was not a make-it-or-break-it graduation requirement. People who are gainfully employed are far less likely to get in trouble or turn to drugs. Instead, they can make a contribution to society and live self-sustaining and more meaningful lives.

In fact, trainers for specific job capacities not requiring a col-lege degree can themselves be trained in high school. Educational tutors are very much needed today to help struggling students with their learning skills, and even more *trained* tutors will be needed for our evolving employment needs. The training program itself creates a wide variety of new occupations to serve future trends. What often goes unrecognized is that some of the skills that may be most in demand in the future have not been monetized in the past. People who are highly dexterous and quick with their hands, those who can readily organize colors and shapes to operate new types of software, and those who have a knack for sound and musical rhythms that create moods for shopping, working, or sleeping—to name just a few of the seemingly "fringe" talents young students may possess—are likely to find themselves in great demand in the future.

I had hesitated to use mathematics as an example of an overemphasized skill because I thought there might be some blowback from educators, but stated the premise nonetheless. I felt vindicated when Elroy Ortiz Oakley, the Chancellor of California Community Colleges—the nation's largest community college system—stated in July 2017, "College-level algebra is probably the greatest barrier for students—particularly first-generation students of color—obtaining a credential...there are more relevant and just as rigorous, math pathways that we feel students have the ability to take." His report also noted that California will need 1.1 million more workers with bachelors' degrees by 2030, but that the college system is far short of that goal. He recommended that community colleges recruit more working-age adults, not just high-school seniors, to qualify for a broader range of higher-paying jobs.

One skill set that will definitely be needed in the future is the one that characterizes *homecare workers*. The *Occupational Outlook Handbook's* December 2015 list of fastest-growing occupations posts home health aides in the fifth highest percentile for the years 2014–24, which could be taught in high schools. People with a sense of deep compassion for others are very much needed to assist the disabled and growing elderly population by completing chores, repairs, and maintenance, undertaking food preparation or delivery service for people unable to cook at home, and many other helping occupations. In the years ahead, there will be an avalanche of Americans reaching old age and an abundance of needs to be met. It is desirable to keep people living in their own homes as long as possible and avoid paying tens of thousands of dollars a month to less comfortable institutions. An army of home care helpers will be needed in the future.

The second through fourth fastest-growing occupations are occupational therapy assistants, physical therapist assistants, and physical therapy aides; ambulance drivers and attendants (excluding emergency medical technicians) are listed as tenth, and occupational therapy aides are eleventh. Although the job requires more extensive training, physical therapists rank eighth. These skills could be taught in community colleges where tuition is low and students usually live nearby and do not require costly housing on campus.

The number-one fastest-growing occupation is for wind turbine service, which is also definitely needed for this initiative as we transition to a clean energy nation. Wind service technicians are currently paid over $52,000 per year, and job openings are expected to grow over 100 percent through 2024. It would be delightfully ironic if unemployed coal miners could be placed in a job working above the ground in daylight and fresh air.

Coal miners and other workers in endangered sectors could become the symbolic canaries—safely let out of their cages to better-paying jobs. Special attention should be given to these areas so they can be an example of the shift from peril to prosperity.

Another much-needed present and future field for employment is human disaster squads. Frequent and widespread fires caused by long droughts, severe floods due to unusually heavy rain patterns, and other disasters such as powerful hurricanes, tornados, earthquakes, and terror attacks—all these disasters require relocating people to safe areas, providing them with adequate food and shelter, and helping to rebuild their communities. These disaster-relief squads could augment federal and state agencies rendering disaster relief aid. Regional areas subject to more frequent disasters might have a concentration of human disaster squads available. You cannot begin to train people to help *after* an unexpected disaster occurs; they must be trained and at the ready beforehand.

Offering training in these areas—in high schools, or for non-students who are interested—is an opportunity to build our service sector. There are many in our society who need or will need help, and there are many others who want to serve and help. Both will benefit from a coordinated program to meet those needs. An additional bonus is that cheaper labor outside of our country or robots cannot replace American personnel in the service sector, which is an inherent safeguard to prevent future loss of jobs.

Many potentially valuable workplace skills have not yet been maximized. There is value in many skills learned from life experience rather than from formal training, such as the experience of being a single parent working a full-time job—experience in planning and execution that would be useful in many administrative positions. Older workers may not have the computer skills enjoyed by today's youth, who have grown up immersed in technology—three-year-olds today navigate an iPod as easily as stacking a set of play blocks. Those skills can be hard to master for many in the older generation, but the lessons learned from a lifetime in the workplace, the family, and community life can help guide how to best market a product or develop and apply new services. The old and the young both have strengths that can complement one another, and both will gain a greater sense of self-worth and be more productive—while giving our society more benefits—if they work together.

The way we will work and live in the future will require many different services than we have today, and the people supplying those services and products must have the skills to do so. Redeployment, employment, and training can provide the means for employment success. Some people may say it's just a dream, or that it's too unrealistic to think our government can train us and help us find jobs. It might seem even more unrealistic for Congress not only to agree on such a program, but to actually implement it. How long would something like that take to accomplish?

Aha—there is good news. It has been noted that our dire need for infrastructure repairs and improvements has been verified many times by both political parties. Congress has also already addressed the vital need for national employment and is to be lauded for cooperating and approving a program to meet these needs. It has formulated a holistic, coordinated structure to provide necessary training according to region and marketplace trends. Most importantly, Congress has appropriated the funds necessary to support this program, the Workforce Innovation and Opportunity Act (WIOA).

With all the derogatory rhetoric between political parties grabbing the headlines, we rarely hear about the good things that Congress does throughout the year. The WIOA was signed into law in July of 2014. It has all the components that were proposed in the RET and already has "2,400 American Job Centers located across the country to assist thousands of businesses in recruiting, hiring, training or upskilling business workforces. The job centers provide information about local and federal resources to assist with business decisions such as marketing and economic development opportunities." The WIOA website also states that they "offer a proven, high-caliber training strategy for workers to learn the skills that employers need for American businesses to grow and thrive in a competitive global environment. Customizable and flexible registered apprenticeship programs match employers' needs to meet employers' changing demands." WIOA also offers to help companies remain competitive by updating or enhancing the skills of their current workforce. They state they also "reimburse employers on a limited basis for the extraordinary cost of training new hires through on the job and customized training" and work with "state and local workforce boards developing sector strategy and career pathways initiatives—regional, industry-focused approach to workforce and economic development that improve access to good jobs and increase job quality in ways that strengthen an industry's workforce."

The WIOA provides employment and training services for adults, dislocated workers, at-risk-youth, and other populations; it is estimated to serve twenty million Americans. There is also an important accountability clause for training providers or employers receiving funds: they must report their outcomes and effectiveness. Congress has tremendous potential for making progress and advancing the state of our economic health, and the WIOA is an excellent example of what can be accomplished when both parties agree to serve the common good.

WIOA can advance this National Modernization Act as it is, or Congress can use it as a template to incorporate conforming components into this initiative and operate it as a parallel program to ensure a skilled workforce is at the ready to modernize our infrastructure. The name of the resulting program is secondary; its function and successful implementation is primary.

There is also an added golden gift of the *funding* needed to research, develop, and implement the redeployment, employment, and training program. That gift is the money, efforts, and time that have already been spent on the working WIOA model.

Unfortunately, very few people are aware of the WIOA program, and funding for abundant advertising for these jobs must be provided in order to make potential candidates aware to participate. The spotlight must be placed on the WIOA and RET programs to bring heightened awareness to those seeking jobs.

The only way to have future job security is to be ready *before* **the job market trends change.**

Whether or not we can bring any manufacturing jobs back, the key to our future success is to create more jobs that will be needed here. Rather than buck the trends, let's be smart enough to anticipate them, especially when they concern our workforce. Let's prepare for the changing times ahead and succeed by being ready with an available workforce at the right time.

There is abundant hope! Our human energy is the heart and soul of the American spirit. Our human energy is a renewable form of energy. Let's get America renewed, repaired, safe, and modernized—for our infrastructure, for our workers and industry, and for our health and that of our environment.

The next section addresses the potent force needed to make this initiative a reality—our *will* to succeed.

CHAPTER 7

OUR WILL FOR A WIN-WIN STRATEGY

There is a feeling in our country that a sharp contrast exists between the rich and established upper class in opposition to the less powerful middle and poorer classes. After an individual has accumulated many millions—or billions—of dollars and acquired as many homes, planes, and exotic cars as desired, he or she must invest the remaining wealth in securities and bonds, real-estate holdings, or businesses. When the middle and poorer classes have to cut back on spending, they consume less, causing businesses and their stock values to grow more slowly or to decline. Rent affordability and home buying are also adversely affected, and property owners and homebuilders derive less profit as the value of their holdings declines.

When more people are working at better paying jobs and can afford to spend more, the upper class and their investments earn more. The result is that the rich get richer—as do the middle and poorer classes. This win-win result is often not acknowledged and generally meets political opposition by wealthy stakeholders who seek to lower their taxes by suppressing spending on societal benefits such as education, health, and welfare. However, a healthy and educated population is essential in order to compete in a global marketplace. A healthy nation is essential for workers' productivity to enhance our economy. Keeping people healthy saves money by preventing minor health problems from getting worse and becoming more expensive to treat. For the poor who are unemployed, a welfare check to cover minimal survival expenditures such as rent and food is immediately returned to the economy, spent in total to cover those expenses. The poor aren't looking for investment opportunities, just a place to live and put food on the table.

The health, education, and welfare of Americans is a necessary investment for our society's future. How best to meet those issues in addition to health care costs and tax reform will be ongoing debates in the near future. The NMA need not fall into the quagmire of buzzwords and sound bites that are kicked back and forth like a soccer ball only to end in gridlock. Instead, the NMA should be recognized as a symbol of a new unified cooperative spirit that will significantly enhance our economy.

The element most essential to the success of this initiative is our *collective will* to put its concepts into action—the collective will of the people and of our political leaders. Congress now needs to act like adults and not like children who spoil the game for everyone if one faction doesn't get its way. A mature adult, regardless of personal feelings, will act practically for the good of all.

Rather than a self-defeating "do-it-my-way-or-not-at-all" attitude, pragmatism and compromise are essential at this time. It is useless to point fingers, but we can certainly progress forward to create a better destiny with our common will and a spirit of cooperation. As we improve the bridges of our infrastructure, we can build bridges between our differences. Great bridges are built when those on opposite sides of the gap reach out to the other side with the intention to meet in the middle. When the gap is bridged, both sides benefit.

There are those who may say that the challenge presented by this initiative is too massive, but the clear and present threats to our way of life are also massive. In his 1960 inaugural address, John F. Kennedy presented a bold goal for our nation: to send a man to the moon and bring him safely back before the end of that decade. Back then, it seemed a stunning vision, very remote and to many people simply unbelievable. Nonetheless, we met that challenge, and we accomplished it *before* the end of that decade. Humankind took its first steps on the moon and returned safely. That was over fifty years ago.

Since then, our abilities to accomplish astounding feats have expanded exponentially. As you read these words, a Mars rover is transmitting important information about that planet after being launched from earth, tens of millions of miles away. That was and continues to be a remarkable challenge accomplished in distant space. Here on earth, we have the knowledge and means to succeed in advancing the status and economy of our nation with this initiative. All we need now is the most critical element to go forward, an impassioned collective will to succeed.

What other alternatives do we have if we don't act? Although many salient points have been made on global warming and air pollution threatening the sustainability of our environment, I hope the following analogy gives a further thrust to motivate more people to act with greater resolve. Consider microorganisms growing in a laboratory Petri dish. First, the Petri dish is sterilized and filled with a nutritive growth infused medium (such as nutrient agar) that supplies the ingredients needed for bacterial life. Then the plate is inoculated with a small smear of bacteria across the nutrient's surface and placed in an incubator at 98.6 degrees. After a day, tiny colonies of bacterial growth will appear on the surface. With each following day, those colonies increase in size and expand their spread. As time passes, the ideal temperature and nutrients provided allow the thriving bacterial colonies to grow and cover the whole surface within the Petri dish.

However, soon after peak growth, the once-flourishing bacterial colonies begin to die off. As time passes, *all* the colonies die off. They become extinct. This happens because as living organisms grow, their metabolic functions produce waste products. At first, the small number of bacterial colonies can easily reproduce, with only a small amount of metabolic toxins. However, once the continued growth of colonies and their accumulated waste products reach a tipping point, the bacteria die off as a consequence of the imbalance that their own toxins have created.

In a sense, our planet has become like the surface of an enclosed Petri dish. Our atmosphere acts like an incubator that encapsulates us and regulates our oxygen and temperature. The earth and its ecosystems supply the ideal nutrients and water to sustain humanity and have done so for an estimated 108 billion human births to date. Anthropologists have surmised that due to high infant mortality rates, unfavorable weather, lack of food, disease, predators, and other adverse factors, early humans had an average lifespan of around ten years. We are now living longer than ever before, and there are more people populating our planet's surface. As a species, we have colonized and expanded around the globe, and like the bacteria in the Petri dish, we have been producing toxic byproducts, which continue to accumulate and adversely affect our health and the ecosystems that support us.

Does this imply that our species is doomed to die off like bacterial colonies in a Petri dish? Perhaps. If we are ignorant of how we adversely affect our environment and refuse to acknowledge the harmful consequences of our own activities, then we may reach a global tipping point like the bacteria did.

But this need not be the fate of our human race. We are not bacteria in a petri dish. We are becoming aware of the ways that our growth and expansion over the surface of this planet are affecting our environment and how those changes are threatening our sustainability. With that insight and with our wondrous ingenuity and creative abilities, we can alter the increasing consequences of our harmful actions and establish a coexistence with nature. Our species can indeed live on, grow, and thrive—if we act now.

There is a song by the late great Ray Charles that I continually listen to for encouragement and motivation to spread this message. Although "My World" came out in 1993, Charles's genius and the prescience of his message convey the feelings that untold numbers of people share today.

"My World," begins not with words, but the plaintive sound of a soul *wailing* out in frustration, dismay, and—uncharacteristically—with an undertone of anger, a burst of emotions Ray Charles can a longer contain. Then his words begin:

The time has come to air my feelings,
There's just so much confusion going down,
I'm not the kind to be complaining,
But sometimes you got to stand out from the crowd.

He declares in the chorus that follows:

It's my world,
Don't you come a messing with my world,
I don't appreciate the fact that some people just can't see,
It's hurting you and me,
It's my world,
My world, your world, our world, one world.

His words resonate with my own frustrations, my own dismay. As a father and grandfather, I have my moments of anger over some of our government representatives' lack of sincere concern for our world environment and how it affects us all.

The bottom line is that it is indeed "our world," and we do have only "one world." The fervent emotion and words that Ray Charles invokes stir my soul and inspire me onward. If you give it a listen, I hope it'll stoke your fire also.

I may be called a dreamer, but as John Lennon said, I'm not the only one. And I do hope you'll join me. However, I'm a practical dreamer. Some gifted thinkers feel that humanity will not change soon enough and propose building space ships to colonize Mars. Space exploration and experimentation should definitely be encouraged. I'm excited to see our rocketry advancements reaching out into space and finding new discoveries. Unfortunately, Mars is a very inhospitable habitat for human life. Other farsighted thinkers envision huge space-traveling vessels with self-contained ecosystems designed to grow plant and animal life in terrarium-like environments as they search other galaxies for a habitable planet to make our new home.

Is that possible in the near future? It would be a very long shot, and the fact is that we will not be able to transport today's population of 7.5 billion people—let alone future global populations possibly double that size—to a more inhabitable planet than we live on now. But we need not build huge space vessels or search the universe for an ideal planet to live on. We already possess a vessel that has all the ideal conditions for us to live and thrive, and it does indeed travel through space. Buckminster Fuller, a philosopher and scientist of our last century, proposed this concept and called it "Spaceship Earth." We are already on Spaceship Earth, traveling through space, and we need not be forced to travel elsewhere.

But we have to use our resources in balance and harmony with nature to keep our home planet habitable. We are far more than mere bacteria in a Petri dish, and we are surely capable of creating healthier living conditions on our planet. This awareness and knowledge is the greater purpose of this initiative. Our collective will is the means to fulfill that purpose—a collective will not just to survive, but *a collective will to thrive.*

Understandably, many people will question whether bipartisan cooperation is possible in today's political climate. Many will ask if collective cooperative action is a realistic goal.

It is hopeful to note at a leadership conference in July of 2017, Republican president George W. Bush and Democratic president Bill Clinton spoke about their admiration for each other and the genuine friendship that they share. They not only respect each other, they enjoy each other's company and joking sense of humor.

It wasn't always like that when they were in the heat of campaigning, it was the opposite. And even though the deep animosities between our current political parties seem unprecedented now, there is hope that this initiative will create common ground for agreement. Then the icy emotions will begin to thaw and a more hospitable environment for growth and enhancement will blossom. Just as past presidents like Bill Clinton and George Bush have yielded to their better angels, so too can the different sides of the aisle get along when they have the desire—*the will*—to do so. They may disagree about certain issues, but reasonable people who truly want to lift up our country's quality of life will use the wisdom of compromise and give and take. That's the way the Constitution of the United States came into being. There were many tooth-and-nail fights needed to carve out the faults so that certain undeniable truths remained. They guided us to achieve what no other nation had before.

It was the *will* of our founding fathers that created the land of the free, and formed our Constitution that has become the law of the land. The will of today's Congress possesses the power to build America stronger and better than it ever has been. Now Congress has to combine their wills and better angels and follow through to make America a country that fulfills that potential.

As the environmental clock is ticking, the heat continues to rise, and our infrastructure crumbles daily, *we need to proceed with speed to succeed.* Not to do so will only present progressive worst-case scenarios. The future is not predestined. We have a choice to direct our wills to ensure our future welfare—or choose to ignore this issue and not act at all. My motivation for proposing this initiative is that the people and the country I cherish will enjoy a safer, healthier, and better quality of life. I hope you share the same desire and motivation and use your will in supporting these beneficial goals and will spread the message through your networks and contact your congressional representatives directly.

Here's how:

*Go to senate.gov and house.gov to find your representatives. Their names, addresses, <u>phone numbers</u> and email information are readily available to make your voice heard.

* Calling is better than writing. Physicals letters are screened which takes time. Emails pile up and are sorted by category; your elected officials do not likely personally read them. *Calling your congressional reps is the most effective way to get your message to them.*
* Before you call, write out a little script for yourself, just a few lines to start.
* When you call, be clear and concise. Tell them about the National Modernization Act if they are not aware of it yet. *The NMA is a bipartisan initiative to achieve clean energy, climate stability, infrastructure improvements, abundant jobs and how to pay for it.*
* Tell them about the part of the NMA that you are most concerned and feel passionate about. You want to add why it is important for them to introduce bills and support all the parts of the initiative as one complete holistic legislative bill.
* You need to communicate how you feel in your own words. Be honest, be yourself, act with dignity and speak politely. Staffers take calls and they are human beings, and your messages is one of many they must handle.

* Call frequently, every day if necessary. Calls from constituents are tallied up and viewed as an indicator of the level of support or opposition to a piece of legislation or initiative. Your representative wants your vote.
* If you write a letter or send emails, follow the same rules; always be clear, concise and polite. Always ask for a response. For more effective email impact contact your representatives local field staff. Congressional staffers are usually based in their districts and states and also in Washington, DC. For calls, speak to their DC office; they are the ones who handle legislation issues.

In a true democracy, the will of the people rules the government—not the other way around. The stronger the will, the greater the influence to effect change. Our current political climate has been acutely activated and continues to grow stronger. Remember, the NMA is intended to be a *bipartisan initiative* for modernizing our infrastructure, economy, and job market and improving our environment for everyone. I believe in a true democracy. Don't give up your right. Do stand up with all your might.

With our nation's united will, we have achieved seemingly impossible dreams. This initiative is far easier to achieve then the impossible.

The next section explains how to pay for the National Modernization Act.

CHAPTER 8

PRACTICAL FUNDING

The last two wars in Iraq and Afghanistan are estimated to cost over $3 trillion for expenditures already spent and for ongoing expenses projected for health and rehabilitative care for veteran's long-term disabilities. Some estimates exceed $6 trillion dollars. In Iraq, we have built roads, bridges, electrical supply stations, and a $1 billion embassy. We have funded supplies, contracted civilian manpower for engineering and construction teams, and taken on a myriad of other costs dedicated to improving those foreign countries' infrastructure and living conditions.

All the while, we have needed—and now *critically* need—those types of resources in our own backyard. Instead of deploying our finest men and woman into battle to kill or be killed, we now can employ our finest to repair, rebuild, and improve our own infrastructure. We can provide training for meaningful jobs. The initial phase of the NMA can start almost immediately with today's shovel-ready plans as the overall plan takes shape.

However, this is a nonstarter if Congress once again says, "Yes, we definitely agree that this initiative is needed, but we can't afford it now." That is not so. There are ways that we can afford it. A legitimate comparison can be made between the costs required for the two wars and for this homeland repair and modernization initiative.

When the horrifying attacks on the Pentagon and the destruction of the Twin Towers occurred, as a nation we reacted with fear and uncertainty. That put us in survival mode, propelled by powerful emotions to take a course of action that hasn't ended well. Acting in survival mode has resulted in the deaths of hundreds of thousands of people and the loss of trillions of dollars. Right or wrong, however, the commitment to spend the money was made.

This initiative addresses not an external threat to our security but an internal one. Unfortunately, this internal threat has lacked the immediacy of attention and funds that an explosive, devastating surprise attack called forth. After all, seeing a bridge rusting on a daily basis or driving over one more pothole does not arouse a sense of urgency. And therein lies our present gift of opportunity: we now have the time to act thoughtfully—with the goal of improving our quality of life, boosting our economy, and preventing hardships and future inflated costs—rather than act in a state of panic, when mistakes are often made. Is far better to act now then to react after a large segment of a rusting bridge collapses and cars crash to the ground, causing unexpected deaths and injuries and a swarm of ambulances rushing to hospitals.

Part of the funding for our country's daily business and for the added expense of the two wars has come from borrowing money by issuing treasury notes that investors bought and receive an annual fixed interest rate and return of principle. This past borrowing has created a burden of debt and has left us with a dubious return on how we spent that money. Issuing National Modernization Act bonds (NMA BONDS) and investing those funds to employ Americans on American soil to repair and create far better American transportation systems and infrastructure, clean energy sources, and jobs, is more than a worthy investment for the future: it also addresses a clear and present danger and *guarantees a beneficial result* that pays a daily dividend to ourselves.

Because global interest rates are now at historic lows, and the dollar is still considered the most desired currency, this is an opportune time to issue these bonds. Economic history tells us that in time our extremely low rate of inflation will surely rise, and interest rates will rise as well, so to issue bonds now and pay them back in the future with cheaper dollars is more than a good investment; it achieves fulfillment of a vital necessity and is a great deal at today's cheap rates.

To begin as soon as possible, $200 billion can be raised with the initial tranche of NMA BONDS. Additional contributory funds for the initiative will come in part from local and state governments, electric utilities, and others. The trillion plus dollars for the NMA will be spread out over a decade and beyond. The truth is that to act now will save money; otherwise, in the future, we will have no choice but to pay higher interest rates for borrowing and to raise road usage taxes and electric utility fees. Future materials and labor costs will also be more expensive due to inflation. One way or another, sooner or later, the needs of this initiative—in whole or in parts—must be met. Working in a holistic fashion is the most beneficial and practical way to go forward. It's time for us to think and act smarter now.

Consider the concept of *borrowing* money to pay bills versus *investing* money. The money borrowed and spent for a bullet or bomb in Iraq or Afghanistan is not recoverable. Once a bullet is fired or a bomb is exploded, it is permanently gone. Funding repairs, improvements, and updates to our infrastructure, on the other hand, is an investment that improves and enhances the value of our country. The money used is a capital improvement, a reallocation of assets to create a tangible product, and the benefits are ongoing.

Think of it this way: you own a home that you have lived in your whole life, and it has served you well. Over time, the roof has developed leaks, the driveway and foundation are cracking, the electrical wiring is faulty, and plumbing repairs are needed. You like your home and plan on living in it for the rest of your life. Suppose the market value of your home in its present state is $400,000. If you do all the repairs, the market value of your enhanced property would be $450,000. If you get a loan for $50,000—which in essence is an investment—and do the repairs, your home asset has increased in value—and, as a bonus, you get to enjoy living in a fully functional home every day. That is a marvelous ongoing dividend.

Another important consideration is that when the loan is paid off in the future, the value of your home with inflation will have appreciated above and beyond the funds invested for improvements. Funding the NMA is the opposite of a non-recoverable expenditure. It is an investment that improves and enhances the value of our nation and pays a daily dividend to all of our citizens without discrimination: better and safer cars and roads, as well as clean air and water, are basic needs we deserve to enjoy.

What if we don't act? In August of 2017 the International Monetary Fund downgraded the value of the dollar. They did so not because our American economy is doing badly compared to the rest of the world, but because they feel that Congress is no longer able to pass legislation to increase businesses and improve infrastructure as it had projected in their past calculations. They had estimated that money spent for infrastructure improvements would have increased our GDP. Not enacting this initiative will retard our gross domestic product and the value of our currency. Issuing NMA bonds and investing it in our infrastructure improves our economy and value of our dollar.

America is our home, and the overwhelming majority of Americans plan on living here for the rest of our days. As long as we are living in our homeland, it should be in the best shape possible.

And you can help to make that possible. Let's make America a better land for all of us!

Other monetary offsets for funding:
The benefits of redeploying and training our workforce, as mentioned, include avoiding the emotional and financial hardships of unemployment and preventing increases in crime and drug addiction. The redeployment, employment, and training section of this initiative will help to significantly mitigate problems of coal miners and other workers in industries across the board being phased out due to ongoing trends of the marketplace.

Another offset to funding this initiative is the savings in health-care costs and loss of productivity due to sickness caused by the ill effects of pollution. As stated before, China is building sixty nuclear reactors to avoid six hundred thousand annual deaths due to air pollution and a much greater number of pollution-related illnesses. The Chinese are thinking ahead and see it as a health and cost-saving necessity, and in the process to reduce pollution China has become a world leader in clean solar power.

Funding for the first three parts of the NMA (transportation vehicles; infrastructure of our roads, bridges, and tunnels; and our electric grid) should not be considered as a significant cost factor because the privately funded automotive industry is already in hot pursuit to be the best and first to offer safe, hands-free cars for the future. In addition, the infrastructure costs for repairs and replacements for our roads, bridges, tunnels, and grid have been established and must unquestionably start in any event. It is a cost we are destined to pay, regardless of this initiative. Clean energy, cleaner air, climate stability, and future job security are basic necessities we must commit to. We have no choice. Avoidance is not an option. We should not live in a state of jeopardy.

Implementing this initiative can create "full" employment for a sustained period of time while raising the standard of living for all

Americans. More people employed add to local and federal budgets with greater tax revenues. People with growing incomes consume more products, raising the profits of companies—which will invest and hire more workers in order to grow in an expanding economy. Greater business profits also generate greater corporate tax revenue, which reduces the need for future borrowing and debt.

This initiative is much more than just a brick-and-mortar project. In many sectors of the economy, new engineering and technical jobs will be created. It will also require innovative applications in a wide spectrum of areas such as auto manufacturing, road building equipment and materials, and new subsidiary small businesses. And, of course, banks will lend more and earn more to aid in private finance for individuals and business to grow...all creating more jobs.

Another funding offset is to give new and updated tax credit incentives and grants to companies and universities to develop new energy resources and advance established processes. The company invests its money in the belief that development of new and better innovations will make greater future profits. The government makes less tax revenue initially but achieves the overall good of advancing productivity for the general economy without paying the full cost to develop the means. As the company makes greater profit in the future, the government will be able to collect greater tax revenues once the credit has been used up.

Tax incentives and subsidies should not be phased out at this time but given to consumers for buying energy-efficient appliances and products such as solar panels, vehicles, etc. We have an $18 trillion economy, and the commonsense goals of this initiative will surely help to keep it growing and thriving. We have the means and the knowledge to go forth. There is no law that prevents us from enjoying prosperity at the same time as we are making our infrastructure better and using appropriate energy sources. We need not make a sacrifice of one or the other; we can have both.

This initiative needs to be thought of paying dividends and saving money while creating greater value-it pays as it paves along the way.

Where to begin?
Your congressional representatives need to formalize the NMA into legislation and get the wheels rolling. Please inform your representatives about the issues in this initiative and ask them to hop aboard and submit (preferably cosponsored bipartisan) bills—or, at the minimum, to approve and vote for NMA bills. As noted before, their phone numbers, e-mails and addresses are available and in most cases you will get a response. When you get a response, thank your representatives for their support; they need your votes to stay in office.

Congress can begin immediately with the committees that already exist and possess extensive knowledge of the vital needs facing us. They have already have discussed and developed ways to meet those needs. A bipartisan overview committee should be created to coordinate the subcommittees in order to make this initiative a reality as quickly as possible.

The infrastructure subcommittee, for example, might present a package for moving forward with their established estimated costs, timelines, and savings offsets. The Congressional Budget Office does objective, politically impartial analysis for Congress on economic issues. It does not make policy recommendations but addresses economic issues such as long-term budget projections and cost estimates for all bills approved by congressional committees. It also issues reports on health care, economic growth, income security, taxes, energy, the environment, and infrastructure. The Congressional Budget Office deals in hard facts and figures, not opinion. The other sub-committees would each submit their package to the overview committee as well. And most importantly, the CBO should work with the ways and means committee to provide funding.

Those in Congress who act to implement the NMA will deserve the support and votes of the public. The spirit of cooperation is essential. Voters should support those in Congress who truly exhibit this spirit to achieve the basic benefits we all need.

These are just suggestions to get things started. There are many brighter and more experienced people than myself who possess the unique wherewithal to bring better ways to the table. I am only one individual, and so are you. The immense power of working together in harmony for a common goal cannot be underestimated and will surely make this initiative successful. No one has to change his or her party affiliation to support this initiative, for it benefits all of us. You are needed.

In our bodies, all of our organs are needed, and each organ depends on the others to function properly. If one organ is unhealthy, it affects our overall health and reduces our body's total ability to function optimally.

Each part of the NMA is also necessary and dependent on the others for our country to function at its best. If one of our vital national structures (our transportation system of vehicles, roads, bridges, tunnels; nonpolluting sustainable energy sources; meaningful jobs; and a healthy environment) is malfunctioning, it affects our country's ability to function at its best.

The NMA presents a coordinated, holistic approach to healing the present dysfunctions of the above vital structures. There is no need for us to be less of a nation than we can be. This treatise is meant not just to be read, but to activate the potential powers of voters like yourself to act. It is also a message for those who make the laws of the land: make this National Modernization Act a law of the land and a symbol of a new cooperative spirit. It is also an opportunity for all present and past governors and legislators to lobby your state representatives in both houses of Congress to submit and sponsor NMA bills. This will help your state to fix and update your roads and boost your economy.

It was federal funding for building and engineering investments in dams, highways, bridges and the like that helped create the extraordinary prosperity of the last century. Now we have to invest again to continue that path to an even greater prosperity.

To quote an American folk song, "This land is your land / This land is my land / This land is made for you and me." Let's make it a greater land for all of us.

With our collective wisdom and *wills*, a better destiny is ours to create. We can and will create a win-win way forward.

Thank you for your consideration and support in helping our country to be the best it can be.

CHAPTER 9

ABOUT THE AUTHOR

For those who may be interested, the following are some of my experiences that motivated me to writing this NMA initiative.

I was born 1943, in Brooklyn, New York. At the age of nine, I moved to Franklin Square, a small community on Long Island surrounded by farmland and a heavily wooded area with a wide, flowing creek. I caught tadpoles in a glass jar and hopped onto rocks to cross the creek on my way to school. My town was about twenty-five miles from Manhattan—today, the woods and farms are long gone, replaced by a density of homes with asphalt streets. The creek has dried up. This was my first experience of city-creep and the disappearance of a natural habitat.

At age eighteen, because of my interest in science, I studied to be an electrical engineer in Boston, but soon decided that I wanted to work with people rather than formulas, slide rules, and a drafting table. I transferred to chiropractic school in New York City, where I met and married my love, a Pan American stewardess. After graduation, I moved back to Long Island to start a practice. At that time, chiropractors in New York were required to pass the New York State medical basic science boards for anatomy, physiology, pathology, bacteriology, and biochemistry. I also had to pass additional boards in diagnosis, public health, x-ray, and neuro-muscular chiropractic techniques, among others.

Starting my practice on Long Island, I also worked part-time at medical centers in poor neighborhoods in New York City. I got along well with the medical doctors there, but many of us felt the management was geared toward squeezing dollars and did not truly address the needs of the patients or the doctors. I felt I could do a better job, and with a loan, I took on the task of building two large medical centers, the Doctors' Family Health Group, and the Central Bronx Family Health Group. The medical centers were modeled as health maintenance organizations (HMOs), with the intention that patients could get all their health services in one place.

My engineering background aided in designing the centers, which provided a complete range of services from pediatrics to podiatry—including psychiatry, dentistry, and much more. They also offered consulting services from specialists ranging from thoracic to cardiovascular surgeons. I was the executive director and coordinated and paid my nursing staff, billing department, and blood and x-ray technicians. I provided the medical supplies and cleaning services. I also coordinated programs with the local community, the public schools, and health department. During a tuberculosis scare, my facility administered tine tests to over two thousand school children in the neighborhood to screen for TB.

The experience of planning and operating the medical centers taught me about the challenges and rewards of working with build-ing contractors, conforming to stringent health codes, securing fi-nancing, and the most important element—establishing the spirit of harmony between my staff of nurses, doctors, and the poor com-munity that we faithfully served with honesty, integrity, first class quality, and a heart. Our nurses and doctors working cheerfully to-gether for our patients created a family atmosphere of healing and helping, which our impoverished community warmly embraced.

I felt deeply touched by the experiences of our indigent patients on Medicaid and their hardships and struggles to—barely—get by in life. Many single mothers who entered our centers holding sick children suffering with fever, pain, and tears in their eyes left with smiles of relief and deep appreciation that we were able to help in a caring way they were seldom treated. I was proud of our entire staff and the role we played in the community.

I also knew how important it was to my employees' lives to be earning a paycheck, and what it feels like as a small business owner to meet your weekly payroll and make sure your staff is paid—many times before I was able to pay myself.

At one time we were about to issue an initial public offering of stock to raise funds to build a chain of family health centers. An underwriter had arranged the offering, and we are all set to go when the bottom fell out of the stock market and all initial stock offerings dried up. At another time, interest rates for a home mortgage was bumped up to 18 to 20 percent in order to slow down a dangerously inflationary economy. It did, but many people were hurt, and many businesses were lost. Mortgages now range from 3 percent to 5 percent. That was one of the many experiences of being involved with changing financial and job market *trends*. I learned to stay ahead of the curve of business swings and be practically prepared.

All the while I was operating the medical centers, I also maintained a private practice. As time passed, I felt my administrative experience with the medical centers had satiated me, and again I yearned to work with people rather than business administrations. I entered into a full-time practice in 1975. I partnered with Dr. Ted McLean, an osteopath in Scarsdale, New York, a classmate of a doctor who became Nelson's Rockefeller's personal physician. After Rockefeller became vice president to Richard Nixon, Ted's classmate became president Nixon's personal physician and went with him to China on his historic diplomatic mission in 1972. When my partner's friend came back, he told us to study acupuncture.

In those days, no one was doing acupuncture except in Chinatown, and it seemed very strange to me that sticking needles in different parts of the body could have healing effects. But upon reflection, considering that acupuncture had been around for five thousand years, and penicillin less than a hundred years I concluded: there must be some validity to that alternate therapy, although at that time I couldn't imagine how it could be possible. In the first foreign-exchange classes, I was invited to study with a small delegation of master acupuncturists from China but had great difficulty in understanding their level of English—as, of course, I would do a very poor job of teaching native speakers in China. Even though I didn't understand the mechanisms of acupuncture, I was able to learn the techniques.

As my studies continued I was fortunate enough to attend classes by a Stanford medical school graduate whose father was a master acupuncturist in China. He was able to synthesize the body's physiology and the theories behind balancing Yin and Yang energies to facilitate healing. A *New York Times* reporter who traveled with president Nixon on his China trip had witnessed the surgical removal of an appendix from a patient whose only anesthetic was acupuncture. Most of our patients were highly educated and very sophisticated in their knowledge of the best types of healthcare available. Many of our patients were on the boards of multinational companies, partners at major financial institutions such as Goldman Sachs, senior executives at various companies, and at IBM and at television networks including the president of ABC, entertainment celebrities and sports figures, especially in golf. What they all had in common was their desire to get well as quickly as they could: they detested being sidelined, as they were in highly competitive fields. They all had read the article in the *Times* and wanted to try acupuncture. Combining osteopathy and chiropractic with acupuncture further enhanced our rates of success and resulted in a longer waiting list of patients seeking appointments.

My experience with acupuncture and Chinese medicine taught me the benefits of being more open minded and not locked into only one way of thinking. That made me a better doctor and able to get better results for my patients.

My practice also included so-called "everyday people" such as the crossing guards at the school my children attended and the sanitation workers who picked up our trash. We treated all our patients equally, regardless of their background. The common denominator of pain and suffering cuts across all economic classes and races. At those vulnerable times, patients shared intimate personal concerns such as critical problems with spouses, children, parents, work, and other everyday hardships many people face. I realized that many of my patients could go to the best doctors in the nation and many did just that in their corporate or private planes. I decided to learn as much as I could about the natural complementary therapies that could bring even greater results to my patients and embarked on a learning program that included hundreds of seminars over the years. Hippocrates, the father of medicine, took his patients away from the hectic city to a hilltop retreat and served them tea and herbs, massage, healthy natural foods, and soothing music. Hippocrates might rightfully be called the father of natural holistic health.

After my partner retired, I opened one of the first holistic health centers in New York and practiced acupuncture, biofeedback, metabolic nutrition, sport injury rehabilitation, healing energy technologies and many other forms of complementary and alternative medicine. I developed lifestyle therapies and spinal mobilization therapy programs, meditation, Therapeutic Touch (learned at New York University), REIKI (when only 12 people in the United States were practicing it) and many other forms of Complementary and Alternative Medicine (CAM) applications. I received many referrals from medical doctors who also became patients. My success treating problem cases continued to improve, and I led many seminars to teach others the techniques I had learned. In those early days (the 1970s), holistic was spelled "wholistic," symbolizing the treatment of the *whole* person, which to me meant heart, mind, body and spirit. We humans are more than just a physical body, we are also emotional, intellectual, psychological, and spiritual beings, and each one of those parts plays a role in our health.

Certain thoughts can heighten fear and worry, which will affect emotions, and our emotions affect our hormonal balances, immune system and overall health. I always tried to incorporate those factors in assessing a patient's needs, and when I could not provide a service needed, I would refer the patient to someone who could. I have noted this background information because in order to be a successful practitioner with my patients, I had to become very sensitive to their feelings and highly attuned to people's needs. That has prepared me to be sensitive and highly attuned to the present needs of our nation listed in this initiative.

It was during a moment of meditation in a grass field when I looked up and saw a beautiful rainbow. A rainbow is created when a beam of light goes through a prism or is reflected through raindrops and is divided into a full spectrum of visible colors. It was a spontaneous "aha" moment for me when I realized that all people are more than just a physical body; we are a full spectrum of feelings, psychological beliefs, and emotional factors that contribute to health or disease. When one part of the spectrum is out of balance and harmony with the other parts, there is disharmony and disease, and when those parts are in balance and harmony, like the rainbow with all its different colors, that harmony creates something natural and beautiful. I felt that each person in my practice was a rainbow of colors inside. My job was to get all their colors (heart, body, mind, and soul) in balance and harmony as best I could. I have tried to use the same holistic approach to address this initiative as well.

The rainbow became a significant symbol for me, and I named my holistic complex The Rainbow Center. I believed so deeply in the concept that I changed my last name professionally to Rainbow. My wife strongly encouraged me to adopt the name Sage as my first name, which I took to mean sage as in the Native American healing herb. As far as its other meaning goes—wise—that was not something that I thought of myself as being, but something to strive for. Until the last breath that I take, there will always be something more to learn, and I hope that I am able to do so.

In addition to teaching at seminars, I also lectured at Columbia College of Physicians and Surgeons' Dental School on holistic studies. I helped to lead a large conference on holistic healing techniques at New York University and conducted a workshop titled, "What Are The Limitations To Healing." I continue to teach seminars periodically and I am certified to offer continuing education credits for professional licensing.

As my children entered school, they were exposed to the outside world and the nutritional values of that time. I became the nutritional consultant for school lunches in the cafeteria as well as refreshments served at Little League games. My wife and I also helped start the Westchester County gifted and talented summer programs. The premise was that all children are gifted and talented in their own way, and that their unique traits should be recognized and encouraged to develop. This of course underlies the premise of the redeployment, employment, and training program—using people's natural and acquired skills needed for the workplace.

I soon realized that no matter how much love and encouragement I could give my children and how well I could provide good nutrition and a safe living environment, once they stepped outside into the greater world they faced the pressures and challenges that all children do when they set out on their own. My children grew up during the Cold War and the overt threat of nuclear war.

Thinking holistically, I joined the Communications Coordination Committee for the United Nations. I wanted to find out what else I could do to make a difference.

On days off, nights, and weekends, I commuted to the United Nations in New York and worked for eighteen years coordinating humanitarian efforts. During my time there I became an officer of the organization and a member of its board. I had security clearance to go anywhere on UN grounds. It was exhilarating and humbling to realize that after showing my ID card and passing through the security gate, that I was no longer in the United States, but on international territory. People who work for the UN take an oath of allegiance and become an international citizen rather than a citizen of their native country. In that spirit I accepted my role there as a world citizen to do what I could to help.

One of the educational projects I headed was *The Global Student Voice,* an international bi-monthly newsletter for high schools that highlighted the United Nations departments and their functions. Topics ranged from building the first international space station, to feeding the world's hungry, to environmental concerns. We also solicited questions and responses from students and their concerns, and George Gallop Jr. was interested in our program. He invited us to his offices in Princeton, New Jersey to discuss how he could work with us and treated us to a delicious lunch after our meeting.

The UN designates each year in recognition of a specific cause, such as The Year of the Child, the Year of Refugee, or the Year of the Indigenous. I became the executive director of the Communications Coordination Committee in 1986, for the Year of International Peace. My goal was to unite nongovernmental organizations with official UN programs that were working for hunger projects, literacy programs, and nuclear disarmament programs, among many others. At that time there were many small, hardworking groups that had very few resources to make their voices heard. I felt that combining all the small groups with the same goals would make their voices much stronger so that better results could be attained.

One of our subcommittee projects was an international poster and essay contest for children and teens with the theme, "Reverse the Arms Race, Enhance the Human Race." The entries we received were remarkable. They ranged from affecting posters to heartfelt essays describing how the world would be a better place if we used the monies in constructive rather than destructive ways. One of the school districts we worked with was the New York City Department of Education, which at the time enrolled over a million students. They were glad to work with us, and we reached many people that year to help raise awareness.

During that time, I also joined the International Physicians for the Prevention of Nuclear War. The personal physicians for President Ronald Reagan and the President of the USSR, Leonid Brezhnev, helped to form the organization. They had the presidents' ears and explained to them the dilemmas all physicians faced with the threat of nuclear war. The book *Last Aid: The Medical Dimensions of Nuclear War*, published by the organization, explains that in the event of a nuclear disaster, all medical knowledge and expertise would become useless. In an emergency, doctors are trained to administer *first aid*, but in the event of a nuclear blast, without benefit of electricity, hospital operating rooms would cease to function. Doctors' ability to offer any aid would be meaningless in any case once people were exposed to lethal radiation poisoning. That connection between the doctors' mutual concerns and their intimate connection with their presidents helped to bring about their leaders' commitment to back off from the Mutual Assured Destruction (MAD) policy and seek a more thoughtful solution. As a member, I was greatly heartened when the International Physicians for the Prevention of Nuclear War received the Nobel Peace Prize in 1985.

With my very busy schedule, I was fortunate to have my residence attached to the Rainbow Center while my children were growing up. I was there for them when they went off to school and when they returned. The school bus picked up the neighborhood children at my office parking area, and on cold snowy days, we invited them to wait in the reception room until the bus came. When my children were in high school, they worked summer jobs in my office. That home/office relationship helped to nurture a close connection with my children that I still retain today.

We were also fortunate to have a year-round vacation home in a very small rural hamlet in upstate New York. The phonebook listed only four hundred residents. I got to know the farmers there and became familiar with the plight of small rural areas during times of economic downturns. When the economy declines, the poor are the first to feel it. They are also the last to benefit when the upturns occur. Regardless of what the price of milk is, dairy farmers must milk their cows twice a day, 365 days a year and provide the feed for them. That experience gave me a feeling for the ups and downs of rural living.

After living for more than half a century in New York, we relocated to California. It was during the move that I sustained a compression fracture of my twelfth thoracic vertebrae, five lumbar protruding discs and two herniated discs in my neck, one on the upper right and one on the lower left. The diaphragm attaches to the twelfth thoracic vertebra, and I felt sharp pain with every breath I took. Because I couldn't breathe deeply, congestion built in my lungs, and when I had to cough, the pain became excruciating. While driving my stick shift car one day, my hands turned blue and white and my fingers stuck together due to the compression of nerves from the herniated discs in my neck. I almost lost control but was able to steer with my knees and arms to edge over to the side of the road.

A few years later, my condition was exacerbated when I was stopped at a stop sign and a driver making an illegal U-turn broadsided my car. Months later, a semi carrying fruit juice lost its brakes and rear-ended a row of cars; mine was the third impacted. That further exacerbated my prior injuries and left me with pain, numbness, and tingling in my hands. I lost sensation to my fingers and was not able to earn a living. Being in constant pain and not being able to pay my bills was a devastating time for me. My marriage dissolved. I felt I had no future to look forward to, only continual emotional and physical pain. I was losing my will to live, and at the lowest point in my life, I thought about ending it. I am writing about this personal experience because I know what it feels like when people lose their jobs after years of being a successful breadwinner. I know firsthand the forces of hopelessness and helplessness that have driven many to suicide.

The only thing that kept me alive was the haunting thought of what my children would feel if their dad committed suicide. What kept me alive was my love and concern for them and knowing they still needed their father. That prevented me from making a fatal mistake. From that turning point, I determined to get better, and I have. Multiple surgeries were recommended, but I realized that nothing is absolutely guaranteed; in certain situations, the condition could be made worse. I had successfully treated patients with even harsher conditions than mine and was able to help them with holistic techniques I had learned. I was the doctor who became the patient. So I followed my own advice and with the natural means and spinal mobilization therapy techniques that I taught others, I have restored my health. I had already known what it took to treat significant spinal problems as a doctor, and now I knew what it meant to be a patient with those problems.

Today, nearly twenty years after my injuries, I kayak and swim regularly and still enjoy working a full day in my practice and teaching seminars. At seventy-four years old, my energy and activity are very good, although I have occasional episodes of painful flare-ups, which occur less and less. When that occurs, I get the appropriate care and take appropriate ongoing care of myself with stretching and living an overall healthy lifestyle.

I believe our country can also restore its vitality and *wholeness*; and that we are presently in an excellent position to do so. We are not hopeless or helpless; we have the power within ourselves to create a prosperous destiny and a healthy environment for all of us to live in. I know that united, together, we absolutely can do it!

From Wall Street to Main Street, from big cities to suburbs to a remote rural town, from the rich and poor, in sickness and health—this is my American experience. It has given me the perspective of time. It has motivated me to compose this initiative. Whatever my experience may have been or whatever my name may be, what is most important is the message contained within this initiative. I am only a mere messenger, one of many who also call out with the hope to make our lives better.

I have lived a good and full life, and now that I know I have fewer years ahead of me than behind me, I hope to leave this world a better place—or, at least, headed in a better direction. I hope this initiative will serve that purpose.

An historic novel also published by author: *Beloved Son: The Untold Story of Jesus Christ—A Contemporization of the Four Gospels. Beloved Son* has received a very favorable recommendation from KIRKUS REVIEWS.

Made in the USA
Columbia, SC
23 December 2018